"A funny, honest, and moving love l[...] we need to know to prepare not just for our children's futures, but our own. I love this book!"

—Jill Smokler, *New York Times* bestselling author
of *Confessions of a Scary Mommy* and founder of
top parenting website scarymommy.com

"If even just the words 'empty nest' make you feel like crying your mama-bird eyes out, take heart. *From Mom to Me Again* is here to smooth your poor, feathered forehead, to say, 'I know,' soothingly, and to offer practical advice for turning your own bereftness into a rich, full life."

—Catherine Newman, author of *Catastrophic
Happiness* and *Waiting for Birdy*

"Don't make the mistake of waiting for the kids to leave home to prepare for the rest of your life. Melissa Shultz tells us why, and how, with warmth, wit, and wisdom."

—Lisa Belkin, creator of the Life's Work
column and the *Motherlode* blog in the *New York
Times*, and author of *Show Me a Hero*

"The kids left, the dog died, and I hadn't spent a moment preparing myself. *From Mom to Me Again* is the guide I wish I'd had."

—Carol Fishman Cohen, CEO of iRelaunch
and coauthor of *Back on the Career Track*

From MOM to Me Again

From MOM to Me Again

HOW I SURVIVED MY FIRST EMPTY-NEST YEAR AND REINVENTED THE REST OF MY LIFE

MELISSA T. SHULTZ

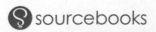

Published by Sourcebooks, Inc.
P.O. Box 4410, Naperville, Illinois 60567-4410
(630) 961-3900
Fax: (630) 961-2168
www.sourcebooks.com

Library of Congress Cataloging-in-Publication Data

Names: Shultz, Melissa, author.
Title: From mom to me again : how I survived my first empty-nest year and
    reinvented the rest of my life / Melissa Shultz.
Description: Naperville, Ill. : Sourcebooks, Inc., [2016]
Identifiers: LCCN 2016001340 (pbk. : alk. paper)
Subjects: LCSH: Shultz, Melissa. | Empty nesters--United States. |
    Parents--United States. | Motherhood--United States. | Self-realization in
    women--United States.
Classification: LCC HQ755.8 .S53265 2016 | DDC 306.8740973--dc23 LC record available
    at http://lccn.loc.gov/2016001340

Printed and bound in the United States of America.
VP 10 9 8 7 6 5 4 3 2 1

To Nicholas and Alexander,
for making my life important.

THERE ARE FEW WRONG
PATHS IN LIFE. IF YOU
DON'T LIKE THE ONE YOU'RE
ON, TRY ANOTHER.

CONTENTS

IT HAPPENS TO THE BEST OF US

You might be surprised to learn that, technically speaking, "empty nest syndrome" isn't a diagnosis at all, at least not within the medical community—it's a *feeling*. Although many mothers who've just sent their children off to college or out into a post-high school world may experience symptoms of empty nest syndrome, such as grief and loneliness, it's not an official "thing" you will find on, say, an insurance form that lists the many health conditions you might suffer from.

As a member of the parenting community and a recent empty nester, however, I can tell you that empty nest syndrome is *totally* a thing, and I can diagnose it with my homeschool PhD a mile away.

Empty-nester moms linger in the very coffee shops we once only had time to dash in and out of for caffeine fixes. Of course we talk about our kids, but we spend a lot more time than we used to talking about other things—like our pets. And we finally clean out the ubiquitous kitchen drawer that went from having a few odds and ends when the kids were born to the one we were afraid to open by the time they left—fearing it would never close again.

Parenting doesn't stop, but it does change. The last time it changed for me was a biggie: I had just taken my youngest son, Nicholas, to college in New York City, halfway across the country. My oldest son, Alexander, was already in school on the opposite coast in Los Angeles, about to begin his junior year. Though my heart was full—after all, they were both on their way to achieving their dreams—it was also broken. I'd been demoted from the best, most fulfilling, most challenging round-the-clock job I'd ever had to a lesser, still undefined role in my children's lives. It's not as if I didn't know it was coming; I just never imagined I could feel this wonderful and horrible at the same time.

If there's one thing I've learned, it's that I'm not alone in my dilemma, and neither are you. Everywhere you turn these days—books, TV, movies, the Internet—the empty nest looms large. That's because around three million women become empty nesters every year. Countless blogs are dedicated to the topic of the empty nest. Women's magazines routinely feature stories about reinvention and what to do with your life once the nest is empty, complete with coping tips from celebrity moms, who, it turns out, feel the pain just like the rest of us. Even Madonna is not immune, telling Ellen DeGeneres on her show that when her daughter Lourdes left for college, it was "an absolutely devastating experience." She was certain it wouldn't be—she thought her sister who had been through it before was just over-the-top dramatic. "And then my daughter left me, and I fell into the deepest depression," she said. The advice from journalists, bloggers, and celebrities runs the gamut from keeping your child's bedroom door closed to getting together with other parents who are going through the same thing. And some of it's good, helpful even. But it mostly speaks to what to do *after* the kids leave.

What about *before?* What about the transition *to* the empty nest? What should we be doing differently so that we're ready for the changes that ensue?

Lots, as it turns out. Not only should you help prepare your child for their new life, but you have to prepare yourself too. And I tried. Oh, how I tried. I read articles, consulted the experts, talked to my kids, made plans for how I'd fill my time. But as it turned out, it was all easier said than done. Once my house was actually empty, the silence was deafening.

From Mom to Me Again is based on my *Huffington Post* blog *The Pre-Empt Chronicles*, where for one year, I wrote about the sometimes funny, sometimes sad, sometimes painful process of letting go of my kids and the life I had known as a mother for twenty-one years.

Through personal storytelling, blogs from my series, and interviews with professionals, I'll show you how to cope with the emotional ups and downs that are part and parcel of the journey, including those related to love, friendship, and marriage. Throughout the book, I'll discuss approaches to the transition that I took as a mother—what failed, what worked, and why—and insights from other moms who are leading active, full lives. Through storytelling comes encouragement, strength, and the assurance that you are not alone. The result will be part adventure, part self-help, and all for the sisterhood—the legions of mothers who are looking for the truth.

Most importantly, the book will explore the process of learning to refocus on yourself, apart from your kids.

As you begin the transition to the empty nest, is it better to allow yourself to go through a mourning process or to stay so incredibly busy that you have no time to think or feel? Does staying busy keep the sadness at bay? If you have a career and lots of friends, are you less sad than moms who stay at home and whose social circle revolves mainly around other moms? Does the transition help you grow as an individual? Will it change your relationships with friends and your partner? What about your career goals? These were all questions I found myself asking, and in these pages, I share how I attempted to navigate them with each new empty-nest experience I encountered. To get a better sense of what's "normal," I talked to experts and some special guests. I also asked women who write about parenting, reinventing yourself, love, and more, for a variety of media including blogs, television, newspapers, magazines, books, and feature films, to weigh in and share their experiences.

By including other women's voices, especially those of professional women writers, my hope was to negate the stereotype that the only people who feel sadness when their kids leave home are women who don't "have a life." It's true that studies *have* shown that the busier you are during the transition, the less likely you are to feel its darker effects. But the stereotype, in my opinion, only serves to judge and blame those who are going through a difficult time. As I've come to learn, while being busy can keep you from dwelling on the past, it can also keep you from making plans for the future—your future. The transition is impactful for every mother, regardless of what else she has going on in her life. The degree to which it impacts you has to do with a variety of factors including your circle of friends, your goals, your outlook, and your resiliency skills. And also, maybe, how much chocolate you keep in the house.

THE BIG QUESTIONS: WHAT WILL THE EMPTY NEST BRING?

It's just after midnight in Texas, and I'm lying in my bed, eyes wide open, staring into the darkness. My husband is sound asleep beside me. The lists I so often fall asleep creating—Mother Lists, if you will—are getting shorter. On this winter morning, just over twenty years after my first child was born, I'm in the unfamiliar position of not being "on call." I can't hear the shower running upstairs or the hum of video games or the thump of a stereo. I can't smell pizza burning in the toaster oven. There are no text messages asking for curfew extensions. It's just the two of us and our dog Benji, now sixty in human years. Our oldest son is away at college fourteen hundred miles from home. Our youngest, a senior in high school, is spending the night at a friend's.

~

I close my eyes and begin to visualize the changes that I know are coming, but up until now, I have mostly successfully tried to ignore.

What's clear in the darkness is that by this time next year, my life will be dramatically different. If Act I was before the kids and Act II was with them at home, I'm headed for Act III: after the kids but with all their stuff still here, there, and everywhere in the soon-to-be empty nest. Reprising the life I had before the kids is not an option—once they entered the world, I saw everyone and everything differently. My heart no longer merely beat—it sang.

A new list begins to form. It's filled with mostly unanswered questions.

- Do I stay in this house?
- What about my career?
- What will I make for dinner? Do I want dinner?
- What about chores? Who do I yell at now?
- Will my husband and I date each other again?
- Will I become a couch potato?
- Can I eat Oreos 24/7?

So this is it—the beginning of the end of Act II. My favorite act so far. The toughest one, but the most rewarding. This is the end of last-minute runs to pick up poster board and required reading. Of cautionary notes from the school about overdue homework, absences, and tardies. Of writing notes to the school that begin with "Please excuse..."

This is the end of the ritual of making breakfasts and packing lunches and saying, "Have a good day." Of family pizza nights and movie nights, of attending school functions and cheering from the sidelines. Of annual doctor visits and childhood vaccinations, of soothing bruises and fevers, of buying cookie dough and wrapping paper and popcorn for school fund-raisers. Of choosing yearbook photos and finding dirty socks under the beds.

This is the end of making wish lists that revolve around being a mom but that never came true:

- Take a cross-country road trip with the family in a Winnebago.
- Take a train trip with the family through Europe.
- Get an enamel pot that goes from stove top to oven so I can

make pot roasts braised to perfection and that don't look like shoe leather on top.

- Get a good set of knives.
- Build a separate laundry room. And tables to fold the laundry on. And put a stereo in so I can dance to Al Green while doing the laundry. And a door to close so nobody can see me dance to Al Green.

And what about time? How will I measure it in Act III if not by school years and summer breaks and pantry wall measurements of every inch my children grow?

How will I manage my time without the framework of raising children?

I'll transition gradually, that's how, and as I do, I'll commit to seeing myself and the future in a new light. That commitment starts now, as I face the reality that I can't depend on the kids to continue to breathe life into mine. Soon, their youthful energy will be gone from this house, and my mom energy will need to be redirected.

Nicholas has finished his last round of college applications, and the holiday season is about to begin. Maybe I'll bake an apple cake and those giant chocolate chip cookies the guys like so much. After all, at this rate, my baking tins are going to end up in a museum from lack of use. Or even better, I could throw a party. An ugly-sweater party where everyone comes and wears their ugliest holiday sweater and eats cake and cookies. That'd be fun. Does it matter that we don't own any holiday sweaters, ugly or otherwise? And that I'm all out of every ingredient I need to bake?

On second thought...perhaps I'll start on that transition commitment in a few more days. Yes, starting Monday, I'll definitely, maybe, start working through my new kind of list (the Not-the-Mother List) so that by next winter, I'll definitely, maybe, be ready and willing to fully embrace Act III with the same enthusiasm I did parenthood. But with a lot more sleep.

NINE SIGNS YOU'RE *NOT* READY TO TRANSITION TO THE EMPTY NEST

Do any of these describe you?

1. Your teenager is your best friend.
2. You make day-to-day choices that concern your teen, for your teen.
3. Your teen tells you everything. *Everything.*
4. You and your partner/spouse spend most of your time together talking about your child/children.
5. You and your friends spend most of your time together talking about your children.
6. Your days revolve around child-related activities.
7. When you think about your son or daughter leaving for school or moving out, you get so emotional you cannot talk about it.
8. You feel as if your best years are behind you.
9. You're thinking about moving closer to your child while he or she is in college.

If you're nodding your head as you read any of these signs, you're in very good company.

PART ONE

LETTING GO OF THE MOTHERING INSTINCT

On Parenting and Loss

H e was sitting in his high chair when I handed him a baby spoon filled with pureed carrots. I'd done this countless times before—watched as my son, Alexander, grabbed the spoon with both hands, only to see the contents splatter everywhere before reaching his mouth. But this time was different. This time, he used his left hand, and the spoon made it to his nose first, then to his lips. I remember this like it was yesterday, not only because it was his first step toward independence, but also because as a first-time mother, I was relieved to put this milestone behind us. There were a zillion more to go, and I had no training as a parent—it's not as if I'd interviewed for the role. I only knew that I wanted it, wanted him, wanted to be his mother. It was the job of a lifetime. But would love and instinct be enough to see me through almost two decades and to see him off to college?

Two years later, by the time his brother, Nicholas, was born, I was in the groove. I'd found great pediatricians, enlisted the advice of other parents, and read many books about parenting. All the while, I continued to work full-time—sleep-deprived, commuting for as many as four hours a day, getting promoted along the way—until what I mostly felt was guilt, for either being away from my boys or away from my job. But the role I most identified with was that of their mother. My husband worked full-time as well.

Something had to give. After much discussion, I decided that my career dreams could wait, especially since it was all or nothing in my particular ladder-climbing workplace—there was zero in between.

So I went freelance and became my own boss. It turned out to be the best decision for my family, though not a great one for my identity apart from being a parent, something I didn't realize until much later down the road.

When both of my sons left for college, I began wondering if I was supposed to stop thinking of myself, first and foremost, as a mother.

I was profoundly different than I had been years before when my oldest child was born. Mothers mature too. Nobody talks about just how much. We start out as undergraduates in parenting, and when all is said and done, we've earned advanced degrees in psychology, medicine, teaching, research, business, and the like. Yet it's the only profession that I know of where so many women who have accomplished so much end up being not only undervalued, but also told to buck up and get on with their lives when the primary job they've held for two decades slowly becomes irrelevant.

It's worth noting that after twenty years of service, members of the military can retire and draw up to half their pay.

I've read studies that say it's all about the marriage—if you have a strong marriage, you won't feel the same sense of loss when your kids leave home. Others say it's about your lack of self-esteem, or the fact that you don't have a career, or if you have one, it's the wrong one.

At times, both my sons' high school years felt like the long good-bye as one routine after another fell away. It sure made it difficult to ignore the loss of a role intrinsic to my identity for so many years. You go from an intertwined, interdependent world to mostly separate lives under the same roof. And all this happens while many moms are experiencing the emotional and physical realities of middle age and aging. You're in this unfamiliar place—a kind of redo of life *before* you had kids, but with an older body and a lot more responsibility—and you're not sure if you're leaping away from your past or toward your new future.

So many milestones had passed since that day my son fed himself for the first time. And as it turns out, yes, that *was* the job of a lifetime, and yes, love and instinct served me well in my role. Which is why I found I couldn't simply flip a switch and get over the loss in an instant.

I know, of course, that it wasn't really a "loss" at all—my boys have matured to become kind, thoughtful, and productive young men. They make me proud every day. But I'm only human and therefore subject to feelings that have nothing at all to do with logic.

The way I see it, until science figures out how to make mothers who look like mothers but are actually computers, who can successfully raise a family by logic alone—and at this rate, that will be sooner than later—I make no apologies for my complex, beating heart.

During my youngest son's last school year at home, I mostly just wanted to try and forget all the rituals that were coming to an end, all the lasts, and fast-forward instead to when he was settled into his dorm. But I'm not a time traveler, so clearly, that wasn't possible. Of course, had I time-traveled, I would've gone backward, not forward—since there were a few chunks of my parental life I wouldn't mind revisiting—for two reasons. The first is that there were so many fantastic years with my children. The time was precious and fleeting, and I miss it terribly. The second is to tell my previous self to stop spending so much time worrying. Because virtually none of the things I focused on actually occurred, and as it turns out, there's a fine line between being cautious and being a worrywart.

The thing about worry is that it takes its toll, sometimes in ways we don't expect. I knew that studies have shown that stress negatively impacts our health, but I figured I was invincible. I ate well and exercised, and my grandmother and mother were healthy and strong and rarely, if ever, got so much as a cold. But at age forty-five, I didn't get a cold. I got breast cancer. My sons were ten and twelve years old.

Don't get me wrong; I don't believe that anyone gives themselves cancer, and it irks me terribly when someone says this, especially to a cancer patient. There's a whole movement out there that thinks we give it to ourselves. And someone actually did tell me this about mine—suggested that's how I got it and that it was my own fault. (This was complicated by the fact that that someone was my mother...and further complicated by the fact that she ended up developing a cancer of her own.) That said, I do wonder if the stress of my particular personality (being the pleaser, the responsible one, and uber tuned-in to everyone's feelings) didn't contribute somehow to my breast cancer having the *opportunity* to grow.

It's funny how a major illness will get you thinking about everything, and I mean *everything*—your past, present, and future. I did a lot of reflecting, mostly about my youth and how, as a parent, I've probably been chasing my own childhood. As childhoods go, mine was anything but conventional. My parents had no interest in living the classic suburban life—the 1960s kind where a husband mows his own lawn, has a nine-to-five job, and balances his checkbook. Where a wife sews and makes mashed potatoes and chocolate velvet cake from scratch. (Two of those three things, by the way, I love to do. Sewing? Forget it.) My father enjoyed being the center of attention and making an entrance. (Considering we were a family of five redheads, that wasn't difficult.) My mother's priority was supporting his dreams.

By the time I was in high school, I was craving some serious parental attention, but I knew my folks were busy with their own lives, trying to overcome much of what they felt they missed as kids. At some point, it occurred to me that I'd spent more time trying to understand them than they had trying to understand me. And therein lay the problem, one that I worked hard to not only overcome but to avoid repeating with my own children. Before

I knew it, my children were young men; one was in college, and the other was a senior in high school, and the lasts were coming fast and furious. Not of the last-in-line, last-to-call, or last-to-arrive variety, but of the end-of-routines-established-to-raise-your-children variety. And that, for me, was a very big deal.

⌒

My youngest son is graduating from high school, and I am, as they say in Yiddish, *verklempt*.

For him, it's an exciting time. It means he's done. He has accomplished his goal. He's on his way to something new. I'm done too. I've accomplished my goal. We feel the same, with one major difference: these lasts remind me of his firsts. He just can't remember that far back.

The last homework: The first was in first grade. The assignment was to draw a picture of me. He nailed it—my hair was BIG. The last was to study for his last final. That was big too.

The last sandwich: I packed his first in a Batman lunch box when he was in preschool. It was peanut butter and strawberry jelly on sourdough, minus the crusts. Beneath the wrapper was a note from me. Since he couldn't read yet, I drew hearts. Over the years, the hearts gave way to words. Today, he prefers his peanut butter naked and packed in a plain, note-free lunch box. For his last sandwich, I honored his request and slathered it on a roll, hold the jelly and the note. Had I written one, it would have said what I thought the moment I first held him in my arms: my beautiful baby boy, I'll love you forever.

The last breakfast: His first school-morning breakfast was a bowl of Cheerios with milk and a cup of apple juice. He talked nonstop. For the last breakfast of his school-age years, he had leftover boneless apricot chicken with buttered, eggless noodles, a glass of calcium-fortified orange juice, and a very large cup of black coffee. He said nary a word.

The last "Are you up?": I've asked this throughout his life. Every day. At all hours of the day. He's had more alarm clocks and backup alarm clocks than anyone I've ever known. Even our dog was an alarm clock. I'd send him in, and he'd sit and face my sleepy boy and bark and sniff his curly head until he woke up.

The last "Have a good day": I said it on his first day of preschool and every day of school thereafter—for the next fourteen years. And I meant it with all my heart every single time.

The last "Please excuse my son" note: The first one I wrote for him was in kindergarten. He didn't want to wake up early, so he was late. The last one I wrote for him was five days ago. He didn't want to wake up early—late again, for the umpteenth time. No more mom notes—I won't be there to write them anymore. So what comes next?

If food is love, I've done what I can to express mine.

If being there every morning to say "Have a good day" is love, I've done what I can to express mine.

If writing "please excuse my son" notes is love, I've done what I can to express mine.

If bugging my son about homework is love, I've done what I can to express mine.

If being a backup alarm clock is love, I've done what I can to express mine.

The last sandwich is made. The homework's all done. The alarms have all gone silent. The dog can't go with him to college. He's ready. I'm ready. Or as ready as we'll ever be.

New firsts, here we come. My beautiful young man, I'll love you forever.

∽

Dr. Carl Pickhardt, a child and adolescent psychologist, author, and blogger for *Psychology Today*, says celebrating lasts, such as with a last lunch box note (if that's your thing), "are great ways to honor a tradition that's coming to a close." Of course, if you're concerned about doing things like this—or perhaps overdoing things like this—he suggests asking your child, say, "I'm still putting these notes in your lunch box—if that's in any way uncomfortable for you, please let me know."

Chances are your teen may secretly love it. That's because in our culture, the pressure to grow up quickly is pervasive. "We are a hurry-up society," says Pickhardt. "Kids are rewarded or complimented for accomplishments that far exceed their years." Sometimes it's because they graduated early, had unusually high test scores, or mastered adult tasks. Regardless, before children are thirteen years old, we seem to want to speed maturity up, and after, we are trying desperately to slow it down. The result can be confusing for everyone, especially if your kids are heading off to college soon.

The Art of Nurturing

Pets, if you have them, tend to become a much bigger part of your life once the kids leave home. In fact, it's fair to say that we moms transfer much of the nurturing once reserved for our children to our pets. And we shamelessly use them as an excuse to stay in touch with our kids. What can I say? It works.

Our dog Benjamin will be thirteen this fall. There won't be a bar mitzvah or a confirmation, but we'll note the occasion with some extra treats and maybe one of those singing birthday cards that he loves to destroy.

I was talking to a friend recently about family, dogs, and my looming empty nest. He's a writer and history professor—smart, accomplished, a father of four grown kids (and from the way he described it, of two dogs as well).

"What's the empty nest like?" I asked him. "What do you do with all the energy you once dedicated to nurturing your kids?"

"You nurture your dog instead. Even more than you do now," he said. "In fact, when your kids move out, your dog's going to become the center of your universe."

He went on to say that no matter how much I think I'm not an over-the-top dog person, I'll become one. And that I should prepare myself for the way the conversations between my husband and I will shift from talking about our kids to talking about our dog.

"Just wait, you'll see," he said.

I know he's smart, but come on—dogs aren't people. And just because I sometimes talk to my dog as if he's a person and say things like, "I'm going to make dinner. Would you like to come help me?" or "Let's go for a ride in the car," or "Do you want to watch *Downton Abbey* or *Dancing With the Stars?*" that's not an early indicator that I'm going to fully transfer the nurturing I once gave to my children to my dog. I mean, my kids are my kids, and my dog is my dog.

I've met people who think their dogs are their kids. They talk about them a lot. Show pictures of them on their phones. Compare dog sickness stories, dress them up, fret about any changes in behavior, worry about getting home to them when a storm is approaching, or dream up vacations that include the dog. Sometimes they even call them their babies. I don't do those things. Well, maybe I do some of those things. Hey, my dog has allergies.

And a delicate tummy.

And he's super cute.

And sweet.

And smart.

Okay. I might be one of those people.

In my defense, I only take pictures of Benjamin so I can text them to my older son. He misses him, and the photos make him laugh when he's having a hard time at college.

And it's Benjamin who wakes *me* up in the middle of the night when a storm is coming and stares at *me* in the dark when I'm asleep until I wake up (how do they do that?), so I can let him out when he has to go.

It's not my fault. He's been a part of the family for thirteen years.

My kids grew up with him, cuddled with him when they were sad, and played with him when they were happy. Because of him, they learned to nurture—to feed and care for him, to be responsible for his whereabouts and safety. In return, he loved them, played with them, protected them.

The year my youngest son was sick, the dog never left his side. And after I had surgery for breast cancer, he was my constant companion. There were days I didn't want to say a word to anyone, but he never minded. He hung out with me through the silence and loved me anyway.

So yes, this fall, when Benjamin turns thirteen and the kids are both at school, I might become an over-the-top dog person. Maybe I'll bake him a doggie birthday cake, get him a special bed for his aging joints, and take his picture wearing a little hat and text it to his brothers (I mean my sons).

Come on, he's becoming a teenager. We might even Skype the guys so we can all be together and watch him destroy his singing birthday card.

Then my husband and I will tuck Benjamin into his new bed and fall asleep talking about how he stills acts like a puppy even though he's the oldest of our three kids (sixty-eight in human years). Maybe I'll even tell a story about something cute he did on our morning walk.

Really, a dog mitzvah wouldn't be such a bad idea.

～

Of course, the primary recipient of your nurturing sans child should be you. It takes some getting used to, this shift in focus. You don't want to go from full house to empty nest in one fell swoop—a pet can really help with the transition. And by pet, I mean anything with a beating heart that you can tend to (preferably something that doesn't talk back, seeing as how you've already had that experience).

A fish, a lizard, a dog, a cat. They all work.

Trust me on this.

The Need to Protect and Control

When I was a kid, before there were shoulder seat belts and air bags in cars, there were mothers with right arms. Mine stuck hers out, palm to my chest, whenever I rode shotgun and we stopped short. For me, the need to protect has always been central to what I consider my role as a mother, and so it has been one of the harder instincts to quell.

~

The parental reflex to protect our children is a powerful thing. It starts long before they emerge from the womb. From their physical health to their emotional, from known hazards to the ones we don't see coming, protecting them is part and parcel of loving your kid.

The first time my right arm sprang out in front of my oldest son's chest, it surprised us both. Thankfully, it was in the car and not, say, at a middle-school dance. And yes, his seat belt was on, we had air bags, and he was taller than me—but it happened anyway. Once I realized we were fine, I looked at him, and he looked at me, and neither of us said a word. We didn't have to—our expressions said it all. Mine was of the "Oh my God, I have become my mother" variety, and his was of the "Mom, you have got to be kidding, you think that scrawny arm of yours is actually going to save me?" variety.

Even for the most Zen of parents, when the time comes to send your kid off to college, it's hard to disarm yourself. At this stage of life, we can only hope they've heard some of what we've babbled on about, what we've role-modeled. Beyond that, all bets are off. They're going to make their own mistakes, and there's nothing we can do about it.

But after so many years of being fully present in their lives, of having eyes in the back of our heads, of putting out fevers, mending broken hearts, and generally being on call, how do you shut it off? Or do you? Do you simply turn down the volume until gradually it's on the lowest protective setting?

This was my theory until last week when my youngest son, Nicholas, passed out cold from the flu. Luckily, he had the good sense to do it at the doctor's office, in the chair I had just shoved under him. It wasn't so much the fainting itself that dredged up my uncertainty, it was the way he looked when he keeled over. The way his eyes, his sky-blue eyes, dulled and rolled to the back of his head while they were still open. The way he looked so completely gone in an instant; the way he couldn't hear me call his name; the way my love for him, frequently tested during these rebellious teenage years, became so powerful, I thought my heart would break. I would have done anything to see his eyes open again. Anything.

"Nicholas," I said, stroking his hair, "it's Mom. Can you hear me?"

The doctor came in, and together, with the help of the nurse, we laid him on the floor. *Ugh, the doctor's office floor, with all those germs,* I thought. Something new to worry about.

"Can you hear me, Nick?" I asked.

"He'll be okay," the doctor said. "He just needs a minute."

"Nicholas," I said, unconvinced, "you fainted, but you're going to be okay. The doctor says everything's going to be okay."

My heart skipped a few beats. Years earlier, after a flu shot, Nicholas got very sick—and stayed that way for a year. Although he recovered, he'll probably always be challenged by some of the residuals. Only time will tell. I know this. He knows this. Is it reason enough to tell him we'd rather he stay nearby next year and attend a local college instead of his dream college far away? Is it reason enough to keep the volume control on high for the rest of his life?

Three days after he fainted, Nicholas resumed classes. I stripped his bed and disinfected every surface that wasn't filled with teenage piles of nothing in particular and everything I haven't been able to find for weeks. While I did, I recalled bits and pieces of advice I've given my older son, who is the opposite of a risk-taker (if you don't count a penchant for Texas Hold'em).

It went something like this:

"Please do think ahead—use that prefrontal cortex of yours to pause and consider the consequences of what you're about to do. But also please know it's possible to overthink, to talk your way out of adventure, friendships, and a career you may have never considered, because in the constant analysis, fear can rear its ugly head and stop you—cold."

Perhaps there is a message in there for me as well. By encouraging Nicholas to stay close to home so I can be within arm's reach, he could miss opportunities to live life to its fullest and to figure out how to deal with his health in his own way, on his own terms. I knew I had to let him go. I also knew I would always worry. But by telling our kids all the truths we've discovered going about our lives, we may prevent them from discovering their own. Although I won't always be there to take care of them, maybe, just maybe, I can arm them in a different way.

∽

When you relinquish control, it's pretty hard to continue to protect your child. It can be scary at first, mostly for you, since your teen probably doesn't know what he doesn't know and is just thrilled to be on his own until he realizes there's a fair amount of boring administrative stuff that comes with independence. I must admit, there was a point in the precollege phase when I found myself looking forward to doing just about anything else except serve as the family administrator I'd become. Anything.

I was cruising along the Pacific Coast Highway (PCH) by myself in a red sports car with the radio blasting, drinking a milkshake from In and Out, the breeze wafting through my hair—

Okay, that didn't actually happen. It was a fleeting fantasy that occurred in the middle of a Target store fourteen hundred miles from home. I was there with my mother, loading up on school supplies for my oldest college-bound son, and I just plain wanted to escape but couldn't.

The baskets held all the basics for his apartment, less the scant pieces of furniture that thankfully came with it. There were pillows and sheets, a shower curtain, cleaning solutions, blankets, toilet paper, hooks that promised they wouldn't ruin walls, printer paper, a trash can, food, and batteries—you know, all that stuff that they never buy but always need.

By the time I got to the register, my mother had, understandably, checked out emotionally. When I attempted to check out literally, I discovered that you're supposed to call your credit card company ahead of time to tell them when you're traveling. Am I the only person who didn't know this? I know it now because they blocked my card, which meant DECLINED flashed on the screen as I stood in line with multiple baskets in front of multiple people. I blinked several times, scratched my head, and tried another card when it happened again. At the cashier's suggestion, I called the number on the back of the credit card, traded top secret information, and provided details of my brief trip, including length of stay and travel partners. It was at once comforting, disturbing, and an invasion of privacy.

By the time we had unloaded everything into the rental van, the call of the PCH was stronger than ever. Too bad my van doors wouldn't close.

Even the kind if somewhat robotic-sounding man in the roadside assistance call center was stumped. Finally, my mother found the one sweet spot on the inside of the van door that released the locks, nearly severing an arm in the process. And no, there were no other buttons, nothing on the remote, nothing on that overhead compartment thingy. It was as stripped down a van as a van can get. But it did have cargo space, I'll give it that.

By then, to say I wanted to give in to my fantasy would have been an understatement. But I didn't. My practical-mom voice—the one that's kept me grounded while raising a family and running a household—took over. I knew I needed to just get on with life and deal with reality, and I knew how to do that well—after all, I am the family CEO. Every family has at least one of me. You know who you are.

Our role is to take care of the details. The skills we possess are a gift and a curse: a gift because we're helpful to have around and we enjoy the process of crossing the t's and dotting the i's (most of the time). A curse because everyone leaves the details to us to handle so they don't have to, thinking we always enjoy it.

Of course, reality is different for everyone. I know people who take regular family vacations even when they can't afford to. Who don't stress about the details of life, or successfully ignore them. I see their Facebook posts, read their blogs. They believe all the pieces of life fall into place by themselves, that it needs no planning and very little maintenance. They do seem happy. But are they happier than those of us who don't live that way? I'm not sure anyone can be that Zen. Or can they?

Not me. I've spent a lot of time doing triage, and as a result, I'm prewired to see the train coming. I no longer enjoy surprises unless they are wrapped in a box with a bow. So I make plans to try and have some semblance of control and fantasize about vacations that I've yet to take.

Perhaps I can expand my fantasy to include one of those body-switching movie plots like in *Big*, *Freaky Friday*, or *13 Going On 30*—you know, where my practical voice will transfer to my kids and their impractical voices to me? That way, we can both get a glimpse of life from the other side.

Until then, there are always red sports cars and milkshakes, right? As long as I notify my credit card company when I cross a state line.

∽

Sometimes life hits you with the unexpected, and the whole notion of control goes out the window. It happened to me when I became the recipient of some pretty spectacular TLC, TLC like I'd never known, not even during my cancer process. It was all I could do to say *Yes, please*, and I learned quite a bit about myself and about life in the process.

∽

When my husband took our youngest son to visit a college out of town, I stayed home. Then my aunt came to babysit me.

Normally, as the parent with a more flexible work schedule, I'm the one who would have gone. But this time, the guys finally got a chance to share a travel experience. So I made plans to have friends over for Sunday lunch. The day after I made the plans, I left my house, drove nearly to my freelance work, and was in an automobile wreck in which my car was totaled. I stayed overnight in the hospital for observation.

When I came home the next day, I became the observer: I saw the pieces of my life, the literal objects I touch on an everyday basis—the shirts on hangers, the items on my desk, the shoes in my closet, all of it—as if I had died and someone else was left to sort through them. It was a wake-up call—me looking around at a half-empty nest without me in it and with a husband who might not be able to find stuff that was well organized for me but not for him. There were systems I'd designed using a shorthand born of necessity. There was always someone or something else that needed tending to, and time was short.

Had I not survived my crash and my family was going through my personal belongings, what would the state of my sock drawer, for instance, say about me? And why did I care? I'd always meant to intertwine pairs instead of rummaging through the drawer each morning looking for two that match. My few nightgowns were a close runner-up—they were turning fifty shades of gray. And my purse...it was beyond shabby chic, especially after the accident. And you know that saying about wearing good underwear in case of an accident? Right after mine, I vaguely remember thinking I was glad I had my better underwear on. And that I had shaved my legs. As if anyone but me cared about any of it and, if I had died, as if anyone would be saying, "She had nice underwear on and shaved her legs."

A week later, nursing injuries and trying to forget the whole dark, twisted, slow-motion series of events, I found myself saying yes to my aunt's offer to come to town and take care of me while the guys were away. It would be a girls' weekend—minus the dresses, pedicures, and parties, of course. Had my aunt not come, I'm pretty certain I'd have never left my bed. For forty-eight hours straight.

Through the years, I'd rarely spent more than a night apart from my youngest son. He wasn't big on sleepovers, and I was the parent who took him places. This trip was important and beneficial for both of us. He had to learn to rely more on himself and his instincts—and his father. I had to learn to focus on myself and not feel guilty about it.

Our house seemed enormous while they were away. All the hustle and bustle that comes with having kids—the routines, appointments, schoolwork, meals, and groceries—stopped. The kitchen went largely unused, save for the making-of-the-tea ritual, followed by the taking-of-a-piece-of-chocolate from the domed glass cake dish, followed by the tea sipping and chocolate eating. My aunt and I spent most of the time lying on couches in what she dubbed the Woman Cave. She understood the importance of the "sisterhood" better than anyone I've ever known. We wore pajamas and bulky bathrobes, rented several movies, had conversations, took naps, had more conversations, knitted (well, she knitted; I watched), did some reading, and flipped through *Vanity Fair* and *People*.

Then, on Monday afternoon, my aunt left, and I found myself talking to my dog. He tried as best he could to read *People* but mostly just because there were treats I buried between the pages.

When the guys got home that night, they seemed to be more in sync than I'd noticed before. They moved in tandem, unpacking their things, doing laundry, telling me stories.

I don't profess to know why things happen when they do, only that this thing happened while I was transitioning to an empty nest and my kids to a life of their own. I now understand, more clearly than I ever did before, that I won't always be here for my kids. And that while I'm still here, I'm going to have to learn to accept what I cannot control and learn to control a whole lot less.

And to hell with the sock drawer.

～

Shifting from Mother to Mentor

Adolescence, contrary to what many parents think, continues until your child's midtwenties. During the years when they are preparing to leave home, the experts say our role does not and should not go away, but instead, it needs to shift to that of mentor—someone who can help them sort out what's happening and why it's happening without making all the decisions for them. The goal is for your children to feel as if they can come to you without fear of disappointment, anger, and judgment. That means both of you have to make the shift, and it starts with you—you have to make the effort to see them in a new light so they see themselves in that light too.

~

When does a boy become a man in his mother's eyes? For some, there's a single defining moment. For others, it's a complex mix of the physical, numerical, financial, and nonsensical, such as:

- When he turns eighteen.
- When his beard grows in.
- When he faces adversity and fights his way back.
- When he turns twenty-one.
- When he goes off to war.
- When he graduates from college.
- When he gets a full-time job.
- When he becomes a father.
- When he asks his mother how she is and listens to her answer.
- When he picks up the check at dinner.
- When he stops wearing basketball shorts to do anything other than play basketball.
- When he no longer wants to save money to buy video games but appliances.
- When he owns more than one tie and knows how to tie it.
- When he wakes before noon on the weekends.
- When he vacuums.

Of course, there are mothers who will never see their boys as men, just as there are boys who never want to grow up—they don't understand the fine line between maintaining a childlike quality and being childish. One is sexy, the other, not so much.

My boys are becoming men. I know because I see them transforming every day. But it's not just their physical appearance that tells me so, though at times, the changes have been startling. For years, I swore they went to bed looking one way and woke up looking another. Nor is it their literal ages, which I still have trouble believing.

No, it's more than that.

Some people say monetary success is the measure of a man. It is a measure, but not of manhood. I've known men who were incredibly wealthy financially and terribly poor emotionally.

As for fatherhood? Any boy who is not sterile can become a father. It doesn't make him a man; it just makes him horny. He can have twenty kids and still be a boy in his mother's eyes—in his partner's eyes too, for that matter. How he fathers, however, speaks volumes about his manhood, his maturity.

And what about age? Is it a mark of maturity? Of manhood?

Nah. There's no magic to the numbers. You don't become a man by virtue of turning twenty-one. No new knowledge is bestowed upon you then by the gods. You're just legal, which means you can get into big trouble if you act like a boy.

No, it's more than that.

For me, a boy becomes a man when he lets himself fall in love. It says he's ready and willing to discover who he really is, to take risks, to care for someone other than himself. And when a man loves with kindness and respect for his partner and himself, it means (hopefully) that as a mother, we did something right—that he learned by osmosis when he was just a boy, even when he stopped holding our hand in public.

And then, even then, when we see our sons as men, sometimes we still secretly see them as our little boys. Because we want to. Not because they are.

~

Kids don't come with instructions, yet we figure out pretty quickly how to nurture, teach, and protect them. I just didn't expect that we had only seventeen years and 364 days to accomplish everything we set out to do before the start of a whole new ball game. Even though I'd been musing on this idea of manhood and how it would change my role as a mother for some time, when Nicholas turned eighteen, it hit me again—harder.

~

My youngest son just turned eighteen. According to the law, he is now, in fact, (mostly) a man (though I'm still struggling to see him that way). I'd forgotten what legal changes ensue when they are eighteen, and how those changes do—and should—change the way we approach parenting and our kids approach responsibility. Turning eighteen is both an emotional and legal milestone. And just as it was when they first came into this world, there are no instructions about how to parent henceforth.

Yes, I know, I've been prepping my child all along for his newfound adulthood. Still, reality has a funny way of creeping up on you. Part of me thought we'd get a package in the mail, an information kit from the government, a sort of "What You Need to Know about Turning Eighteen" type of thing. It's not a bad idea, though admittedly, a tad creepy. When my grandmother turned one hundred, my family got a letter from the president.

In the absence of government mail, I did some research, which I followed with ibuprofen for the ensuing headache and eight episodes of *The Big Bang Theory* because I needed to laugh again.

Although an eighteen-year-old can't drink legally (hence the "mostly" of the "mostly a man" comment above), he can vote, fight for his country, serve on a jury, buy a house, get married, and get arrested.

I am no longer the legal representative for his health, unless he grants me permission. I can, however, keep him on my health plan until he's twenty-six.

I cannot, without his consent: discuss his credit card bill with the bank, even though I am his cosigner (and even though he doesn't have one yet); discuss his tuition bill with his college, even though I am mostly paying for school; or view his grades, even though, again, I am mostly paying for school.

In my new role, I am a consultant on call who still supports him financially and makes his dinner. Okay, I didn't find that last part online, but let's be honest—that's the way it is. At least until he starts college.

Of course, he still acts like a teenager: throws his laundry on the floor, waits weeks to wash his linens, has mood swings, negotiates curfews (I no longer have legal control, but he knows who pays his car insurance), and stays up too late doing homework that he should have completed earlier but fell asleep instead. And I love him anyway.

So besides reading up on the facts, I'm trying a new approach to help combat the emotional response I get every time I look into his baby blues. We'll see how it works. I'll:

- ask "How can I help?" instead of telling him what to do.
- let go of any preconceived notions about the choices I think he'll make based on his childhood.
- get busier with my own life so I don't focus on the inevitable screwups quite as much.

- remember that I'm still in the game. I just moved from pitcher to catcher—he's the one who's up to bat.

Blogger Becky Galli (http://www.rebeccafayesmithgalli.com/), a single mom of four (two of whom had special needs) who was left paralyzed after a rare illness in 1997, has remained an active and involved parent now that her kids are grown. At first, she did feel as if she had lost her job and says it can be sad at times: "It's the same sense of loss that I felt when I resigned from IBM after ten years in marketing and sales. I loved my job, but it was time to be home full-time with my kids. Many who left IBM came back in as consultants on an as-needed basis. That's how I feel about parenting these days. I'm still their mom, just more of a consultant… So I don't regret one minute of how I spent my parenting career. That joy far outweighs any sorrow I feel."

For moms who feel they've made sacrifices for their kids and that those sacrifices have impacted their lives in negative ways, the shift to mentor can be helpful.

What are the implications of parental sacrifice? How does the very notion of it affect parent and child? "At worst," says Carl Pickhardt, "parents can feel resentment at the end, while departing kids can leave feeling guilty about sacrifices made on their behalf."

Sometimes the resentment can be a wake-up call for parents, a clue to begin to refocus on themselves. The goal, of course, is to avoid getting to that point to begin with—where you are angry and hurt for what is actually a normal stage of child development. Experts say the guilt your son or daughter feels as a result of the resentment you communicate will not be helpful for your future relationship, one in which you have the opportunity to become a mentor.

So how do you avoid falling into this sacrifice pit? Again, start the process of separating before they have one foot out the door. Yes, this is tougher than it sounds; we spend the first decade of their lives making sure they feel a sense of attachment to and security with us, and it can be hard to let go, especially when we truly enjoy being with them. So timing here is everything, and paying attention to the signs that they are ready to mature is key. Most kids begin to pull away from us between the ages of nine and thirteen because they want to be more adult. The first thing you might notice is that they won't let you hug them or hold their hand in public, or they'll ask you to drop them off near instead of at their destination so their friends won't see you. It's all good, even though it feels bad, and I know from both experience and research that if these things happen, it generally means you've done your job right. The strong attachment foundation you established is giving them the confidence to start becoming more independent and to develop as an individual. What's critical is that parents convey to their children that by allowing them more independence, you are not in any way pulling back on your love or abandoning them.

This can be an especially emotional stage of parenting as we struggle with the concept that we are setting our kids up to fail. Dr. Pickhardt suggests making a change in your thinking from "We are responsible for you and regulating your actions" to "We accept that you make your own decisions and that you must deal with the consequences." To accomplish this, try cutting back on the decision-making, particularly in the year or two before your son or daughter leaves for school. The same goes for solving problems. "Your teenager is going to come up against obstacles: teachers who they think may not be 'fair,' challenges with friends," says Dr. Jennifer Hartstein, a child, adolescent, and family psychologist. If you swoop in to save the day each time, your teen will never learn how to save their own day. That's not to say you can't help, but let them take the lead.

Remember, a gradual process of separation and transition is best. Teens still need you to help them learn *how* to be independent. Although they may get by if you don't transition gradually, it doesn't mean they've learned the skills they need to become successful adults.

Psychologist and writer Dr. Margaret Rutherford believes the best way to transition to an empty nest or any new stage of parenting is to move along with your child. That is, to not look back, only forward. To achieve this, she says you have to "relish and let go. Every stage of a child's life is a fantastic opportunity to practice what the empty nest will bring you, just in smaller doses. If you truly relish each stage and do the things that will bring you satisfaction and contentment, you should be able to move with her... If you do this all along, you can transition to the empty nest pretty well, because you've been practicing."

I don't recall my mother spending any time talking about the empty nest when I was growing up. Still, just when I least expected it, she helped me transition to my own.

~

This Christmas, the last with our youngest still in the nest, my Jewish mother celebrated the holiday with us for the first time. It was, in fact, the first Christmas she's ever celebrated. Other than birthdays, the only previous gift-giving she'd experienced was during Chanukah, when the presents were practical—of the flannel nightgown, wool socks, and cotton underwear variety. I think we even gave her a toaster one year, and she pretended to like it.

I'm not saying Chanukah wasn't fun for us. After all, we sang songs, played dreidel, and ate a lot of potato pancakes. But once my Catholic boyfriend (now husband) included me in his family's Christmas gift-giving ritual...once we got married and had kids and I learned to create Santa footsteps made out of flour that led to the fireplace and the plate of cookie crumbs that proved Santa slid down the chimney...once I waded through mud and helped cut down a live tree and tied it to the roof of an old truck to haul it home...once I tasted hot cocoa after cutting down that tree, then decorated it...once I saw how fun it was to give someone something they wished for, as opposed to giving them something they needed—it was pretty hard to go back to flannel and wool and cotton.

My husband and I merged the holidays to give our kids a sense of both their parents' traditions, and yes, because it was more practical. So on this snowy Texas Christmas day at noon, my sons, Nick, now seventeen, and Alex, twenty, gathered with my husband and me on the floor around our little Chanukah bush along with our dog, who has become the chief unwrapper in the family and pursues his job doggedly.

We gave my mother a chair to sit in, which she assumed was a director's perch until she began to receive gifts and realized she was wholly unfamiliar with what was unfolding. We hadn't told her ahead of time that we'd be exchanging gifts. I suppose it was partly because I felt guilty about merging the holidays, partly because it would be like trying to explain a feeling to someone who has no experience with it, and partly because we wanted to surprise her and not make her feel she needed to do something in return.

After a lifetime of guarding her feelings, holding back, thinking she was supposed to be in the role of educating everyone, and rarely sharing her own stories of trial and error, parenting, friendships, and love, she finally let herself just be and enjoy the ride. And so I did too. Sure, there were a few "You shouldn't have done this" and "I wasn't expecting this" comments, but I paid them no mind.

There were no big gifts exchanged, just acknowledgments of each other's interests. Some gifts were homemade, some store-bought, but all were related to things we enjoy doing and that make us who we are or are hoping to become. It's an acknowledgment that we are in tune with one another and respect each other's individuality.

Our youngest son, the one who used to be easy to read, then became a teenager, was also enjoying the ride—he was grinning from ear to ear. Our oldest son, a sophomore in college who sees and feels everything yet has a Spock-like logic and is now nearly a man, had a newfound serenity about him. Perhaps it was the satisfaction of buying gift cards for his parents using money he and his brother earned, a gesture that took us by surprise and made me well with tears. Then again, perhaps he was just sleepy—noon is, after all, early to rise for a college student on Christmas break. Little children often like the boxes of the gifts they get more than the toys inside them; it would have been enough for this grown-up if they had just given us the envelope they put the cards in, the one they hand-addressed to Mom and Pop using a fat-tipped Sharpie, the Sharpie I once used to write their names on their new school supplies.

And to think that up until this year, the year before our empty nest, I'd never thought of blending my mother's world with ours during the holidays because I was worried about what she might think or say, worried that she wouldn't approve of or understand what we do and how we have decided to do it over these now twenty-one years of marriage.

And so here we are, on the eve of the New Year, a year that will be all about saying good-bye to the old way of doing things and hello to our new stage of life. A year in which I need to accept that the traditions that revolved around my children can evolve and yet still be meaningful and intimate. And isn't that what it's all about, really? When your kids move away, you mourn the loss of those traditions and the intimacy of your family unit. The world you created for them, took pride and comfort in, has ended.

I'm glad my mother was here for the holiday. She provided a welcome distraction and comfort to me especially.

Hopefully, my children will remember that it's always worth the extra effort to renew and strengthen family ties. And that there's something about mothers and transitions.

~

Talking to Your Kids

As you continue to shift responsibilities and roles during the last years of high school, be sure to initiate an honest dialogue with your kids. Something along the lines of "This is all new for me, as I know it is for you. Our roles are changing. We need one another differently, and we have different expectations about how we should be interacting during this shift to your adulthood. Let's be patient with one another and honest in a kind way. I'll tell you when you've crossed the line, and please do the same for me."

I had this very talk with my own kids. It began with my oldest when he got upset about something I said to him during his freshman year. Much to my surprise, he reacted well to the conversation, as did his brother when I had the same talk with him. Really, the discussion took the pressure off all of us—it was an acknowledgment that they were maturing and that we are all imperfect.

It's also a good time to tell them a few truths and resulting lessons learned from your own growing up (experts call this "self-disclosure")—it might help provide perspective if they are going through similar challenges and encourage them to talk. Of course, you don't want to scare them to the point that they are afraid to try things, and striking the right balance can be tricky. Dr. Jennifer Hartstein suggests that you preface your stories not with doom and gloom but more with, "Hey, just wanted you to know about this…" Another approach, and a very effective one, she says, "is to have open-ended conversations about what *they* think is going to happen when they go to college (or head out on their own) and to problem solve all sorts of scenarios that they might encounter." When they do encounter issues (and believe me, they will) and ultimately work to resolve them, Hartstein says to try, "I'm so thrilled with what you did, and so proud." You'll find that it not only encourages them to make good decisions, but also encourages *you* to keep honing your new role in their lives.

Keep in mind that it can be difficult to gauge your son or daughter's emotional growth when you're with them day to day. Often, it's not until they've been away—then return home—that the maturity becomes more evident.

~

When I was little, I wanted to be *That Girl*, from the TV show starring Marlo Thomas. In my twenties, I moved to New York and set about to define my career and conquer the city. It worked for a while, but before I knew it, I was married with children, living in the Maryland countryside, and driving a minivan.

I'm back to square one now. I've learned plenty along the way, so much so that if I were able to go back in time and take something nonmaterial with me, it would be the knowledge I've accrued about relationships and careers. That said, I know there are no guarantees I wouldn't have made the same mistakes twice. Conversely, if I were to leap forward from my twenties to today and bring something with me, it would be my younger self's sense of wonder. It's not that I'm jaded exactly or that I don't look forward to new things, it's just that the level of joy I feel at this stage of life might be compared to the lowest setting on a fan, and it's not enough to cool me. Luckily, the past and the present sometimes converge in unexpected ways.

Last weekend, on a cold and snowy Saturday evening, my husband and our teenage son, in New York to visit a college to which he was accepted, strolled the busy sidewalks of Times Square. They came upon tourists and Disney characters, Spiderman with a fanny pack, a man painted in gold and carrying a golden cardboard ATM box, and a night sky lit up by the glow of giant neon signs. The soundtrack to their evening spectacle was a cacophony of voices, car horns, and street musicians. It was far from the suburban landscape of our son's middle-school years and light-years from the countryside he had known before that. My husband saw him take it all in, watched him forget it was frigid and his boots were wet and he was a self-conscious teenager, and let him just be. And while our son was looking here, there, and everywhere, his father recorded an image of him.

The moment I saw it, I was transported. The expression on his face was my expression twenty-seven years ago. Not only did it thrill me—after all, my college-bound kid was happy, engaged, and aware—but when I saw him against that New York City backdrop, I thought, it's That Boy. That Girl had a baby who grew up to be That Boy, which now makes me That Woman, and maybe I've still got some career defining and city conquering of my own to look forward to.

And I didn't even have to time travel.

It's a Process, This Separation Thing

It wasn't the last trip my husband and son would take without me. There was one more, several months later—a repeat of a trip I had made with my son the summer before when he was just starting to look at colleges. I felt odd about not going this time but was still recovering from the car accident, and as it turns out, sometimes a little time at home on your own is the best medicine.

⌁

My family has gone away and left me home alone for the weekend. Borrowing two expressions frequently heard from the teenagers who visit my house on a regular basis, it feels totally weird and makes me want to LOL. And by that, I mean I have no idea what I'm going to do first, because I am somewhere between giddy and uh-oh.

When my oldest son left for college, my routine was adjusted—I subtracted a few responsibilities that he soon acquired himself. This spring weekend, with my husband and youngest son out of town, I'll get an even better sense of what life will look like come next fall when both my sons are away at school. Clearly, I'm going to have some time to fill...or to readjust...or both. So I listed several ways I might spend my precious two days and nights alone:

- I could tap into my domestic diva persona and organize overflowing closets and drawers and photos that nobody looks at anymore.
- I could explore my inner girlie-girl and go window shopping or try on clothes and shoes for two days straight. Or until I'm hungry. Especially since I know I will get hungry long before the two days are up.
- I could have a party. I think we still have our very old, very large, wooden Bose speakers. They use those at parties, don't they?

- I could eat out when I want, where I want, any time of the day I want. I could forgo meals and just eat snacks and drink milkshakes, and nobody would be able to hear me slurp those last delicious molecules.
- I could give myself a pedicure.
- I could spend the weekend at the library reading and not say a word to anyone.
- I could pretend I'm in Hawaii at a writer's conference where it's warm and there's a breeze and just write, write, write.
- I could take up painting.
- Or singing.
- Or maybe I could stay in my bathrobe all weekend.
- And talk on the phone.
- And watch all the TV shows I've missed over the years.
- I could do a little bit of everything and a big bit of nothing.
- I could stop saying "I could."
- And start saying "I will."

I will remember to give myself permission to do things that have nothing to do with being a mom and everything to do with me rediscovering how to be me. And I will learn to be okay with that even if it makes me feel totally weird and want to LOL.

I will.

~

Although mothers often feel selfish for asking for time away from the family, it's very important to have some downtime. Too often, mothers end up being everyone's caretaker, but they don't meet their own needs. "Unfortunately," says Hartstein, "in not modeling self-care, mothers burn out and continue to be asked to put themselves last. If mothers can put themselves first, they are actually more present for everyone else." Moms are also often the first to give up their personal plans when their teenagers announce they're hungry or want something taken care of. Unless it's an emergency, it's important for moms to keep to these plans. Dr. Hartstein says that one word can make a big difference: *and*. Be sure to tell yourself, "It's true they need me, *and* I deserve to do the things that I want," as opposed to, "It's true they need me, *but* I deserve to do the things that I want." *But* begets an argument; *and* empowers and serves as a reminder that we can suggest options for our children and keep moving ourselves out the door.

So what did I end up doing with my weekend alone? The pedicure was the easy answer. Apart from that, not much else happened that didn't involve old movies and meals of toast and eggs. The *I could* aspect of my weekend got overwhelming. By the time I was done imagining, I realized I was tired and just wanted to be still. Don't get me wrong—I enjoyed having my own schedule. In fact, I'd forgotten just how much I enjoyed it. And that, in a nutshell, was the lesson learned. It only took me nineteen years to figure out that time alone was time well spent and that I hadn't allowed myself enough of it.

Transitioning to an empty nest takes patience, guts, and introspection. To get through it, keep telling yourself:

1. Apply Dr. Rutherford's "Relish and Let Go" concept. Relish each stage of parenting and move on to the next—the goal is to transition as a parent at the same time your child is transitioning to adulthood.

2. From here on in, there are things that you will not be able to control about your child's life and future.

3. You have faith in your children—you raised them right and gave them the tools to make the right decisions.
4. You have faith in yourself and will move forward and embrace whatever comes next.

When you forget this stuff (and you will), repeat steps 1 through 4.

Of course, there will be days when you think you're fine, then the littlest thing will trigger an unexpected memory, and you will turn to mush…

~

He walked into the kitchen, and it took a moment for my brain to process that something was different…to understand why his expression reminded me of when he was a baby and why his cheeks looked so pink. And when I did, I got weepy. I'm not sure who was more surprised at my reaction, me or him.

My youngest son, the boy who spent his childhood laughing and entertaining our family—he shaved off his beard. The beard that he'd worn for nearly a year and that seemed to age him and make him appear more serious overnight. And just like that, the boy I remembered was back and standing right in front of me. He'd probably been thinking about shaving it off for weeks, then woke up and did it without a word to anyone—his spontaneity being one of the things I love about him and worry about the most. So there he was, waiting for me to notice, and in that instant, he became my baby again, playful and mischievous. My baby who is not really a baby, who's headed off to college in a matter of weeks.

And so I cried.

I know. Buck up, you say, that's how it works. You raise your kids to be independent, then they move away—head to college or start a career. I should be happy he's not staying at home doing nothing. And I am, of course.

But let's be honest—it's a process, this separation thing. For both the parent and (former) child. It took eighteen-plus years to get here, and by "here," I mean to the point in parenting when all the many stages of child-rearing and growing up have been crossed off the list. All the predictable stages, regardless of how individual they may have been: from a child's first laugh, first word, first step...the braces, illnesses, wisdom teeth...the wins and losses, driver's tests, dates...the SATs, the college applications, and straight on through to that final day when they wear their cap and gown.

There's a trunkful of memories. A wealth of nuances, family experiences, words, and laughter. So many stories that are by themselves unremarkable, but together are meaningful and the story of our lives so far. And yes, there are more to come, but not the same kind of stories—in the same house with the same dynamic—with each of us in our set role before we make the big shift to the future us.

So no, I don't want to buck up. Not yet. Give me time. And I'll do the same for you—all you parents in the same stage of life.

After all, just because they're becoming adults doesn't mean they're not still our babies.

∿

To ease my angst about the transition, I took a lot of long walks. Every step was a visual reminder of the importance of moving forward. Of how you can't get from one place to another instantly, that you have to go through a process—and like any process, the transition takes time, commitment, and in this case, a decent pair of sneakers.

~

Recently, while out for a walk, I was able to lift my serious mood when I ran into a friend, a mom of six, driving her well-used Suburban. She called out to me, "I love your column."

"Thanks," I replied, surprised not only because she pulled up behind me (of course I was wearing my ugliest clothes), but because I didn't know she read it.

"I don't think I'm ever going to have an empty nest," she said. "My kids keep coming back home." She gestured with her left hand, completely engulfed in gauze. It looked like a boxer's mitt in white.

"What happened?" I asked.

"I was opening a can and cut two tendons in one of my fingers. I had surgery, and now I'm going through physical therapy."

She had me at tendons. Anytime anyone mentions them in the same breath as cut, I imagine blood splattered everywhere like in a scene from *CSI* or *Bones* or that skit from *Saturday Night Live* where Dan Aykroyd is playing Julia Child: she cuts her finger, and fake blood comes squirting out while she keeps cooking.

Like Julia, I know this mom can whip up a meal for a crowd, my youngest son being one of that crowd in years past.

"I guess with everyone back at home," I said, "you're doing a lot of cooking, opening a lot of cans."

"Yes," she said, "and at this rate, I think I'm going to have to be the one who moves out. They're driving me crazy."

I hear that many parents' empty-nest plans are being put on hold. Between the economy and the job market, things are changing.

All I know is the conversation got me thinking about two things:

1.   I need to open cans more slowly.

2. There's some stuff I won't miss when they do move out. Take, for instance:

Sandwiches. Please, take them. I learned early on that kids like "gross" sandwiches, but there's cool gross and uncool gross. Make them a peanut butter and jelly sandwich layered with tortilla chips, and they make new friends; make them a smelly egg-salad sandwich layered with tortilla chips, and nobody wants to sit next to them. By the time mine were in high school and many of their friends were leaving campus to buy fast food, I made a deal with the devil: I promised to keep making their lunches if they promised to eat them. I figured I'd pack leftover dinner and we'd be done. Turns out that's just flat-out uncool.

What did they want? Sandwiches. After making thousands of them, there are no variations on the lunch box favorite I haven't tried. From white bread to wheat, from rolls that are square to rolls that are round, to raisin bread, tortillas, pitas, lavash, biscuits, and more—if it exists, I've slathered it with spreads, butters, jelly, and dressing; filled it with meats, cheeses and vegetables; and cut it every which way from Sunday.

Well, maybe there is one I haven't tried but did seriously consider when my children were growing faster than the speed of light and I could not fill them up: a spaghetti hoagie. The only thing holding me back was Dr. Oz and an irrational fear that he'd show up at their school, see the sandwich, move in for a close-up and ask, on national TV, who their mother was.

Laundry. After twenty years of trying, I still have no idea how to fold fitted sheets. I sort of close my eyes and mold them into a shape. As for the kids' clothes, years ago when Target was having a blowout sale on the ugliest plastic laundry baskets you have ever seen, I bought six. It happened somewhere around the time my kids started putting their own laundry away, a.k.a. the time they started using laundry baskets as drawers. That's when I told myself that if they didn't care how wrinkled they looked, I needed to stop caring how wrinkled they looked.

The wormhole. My mother had one too. "Have you seen my...?" she'd ask. In science fiction stories, a wormhole moves someone between distant points in space-time; in my house, it moves homework to folders that I find when I'm doing my taxes, books to food cupboards, dish towels to sock drawers, and socks to who knows where.

Carpetbag purses. For two decades, I've been envious of anyone carrying a purse smaller than a breadbox. If you're a mom, you know what I mean. It worked for Mary Poppins, but she must have had a personal trainer, because my arms are getting really tired.

Yes, in my empty nest, I'll have a smaller purse and a lot less laundry. In memory of my two kids, I think I'll make a spaghetti hoagie.

Unless, to my great disappointment, it disappears into the wormhole.

～

When It Really, Truly, Finally Happens

Kids move out emotionally at least a year before they do physically. And it's important to remember that it's mostly a one-sided thing—we're the ones who are left behind with memories of them in every corner. As far as leaving us is concerned, in their minds, we're *always* here—they know where to find us.

Drop-off stories run the gamut—with my oldest son, I made the mistake of turning around and looking back when we said good-bye. I do not advise this.

Broadcast journalist and mom of three Jane Pauley was surprised to find that taking her twin son and daughter to college was different than she expected. "It was an adventure we shared right up to the moment it was clear that my part of the adventure stopped and theirs kept going. We deposited our son first and his twin sister a week later. I was obsessed with organizing his stuff. My son's T-shirts were left folded and organized by prints and solids and color. I'd never done this at home. I was under his desk untangling electronic cords and attaching twist ties to keep them neat when I sensed he and his new roommate silently agreed the time had come for Mom to go! It was so obvious the kids were eager for us to leave, I left without anxiety. My daughter started college a week later. I made her bed while the dads were fumbling with shelves and technology. She was very sweet about holding my hand (in public!) as she walked me to the car! She'd told me something a year before that she'd learned in high school psychology: 'The empty-nest syndrome lasts about a week.' We still had their little brother and his friends at home, so it was not exactly an empty nest yet. Still, it was a lot easier than it was made out to be."

Georgette Adrienne Lopez, mother of twin sons and a lawyer and producer who works in the television industry, had just finished moving the second of her boys into his freshman dorm when she began to drive away. As she looked into her rearview mirror, she saw him waving good-bye, teary-eyed and holding a small box containing some of his things from home. For Lopez, a divorcée who took care of most of her sons' upbringing, seeing him standing there, his image getting smaller and smaller until it disappeared altogether, unleashed a flood of emotions. "That was it," she says. "I was a hot mess."

Up until that moment, Lopez had considered herself an optimist, even after she lost her full-time job several years before. "I figured if I just kept going, I didn't have to focus on it." As the reality of the looming empty nest began to set in, Lopez knew that she needed to face some truths—chiefly, that she had been "faking the funk" for many years, and that for herself and her sons, she needed to focus on the open road that lay ahead.

Beverly Beckham, mom of three and *Boston Globe* correspondent whose popular essay "I Was the Sun, and the Kids Were My Planets" has run every year since it was first published in August 2006, says she and her husband, along with their oldest daughter, who had already graduated from college, drove their youngest to school for her freshman year. When they arrived, there were signs on the RA's door for free condoms, and then she witnessed a drug deal before having to leave her daughter in her dorm. "I cried all the way home," she says. "My twenty-three-year-old daughter was in the back seat pretending to be a princess kidnapped by deranged people—she was trying to make me laugh." Beckham says it seems like she must have cried for weeks, and then one day, her daughter called and told her how unhappy she was at school, and everything changed. "I wanted her to be okay," says Beckham.

Over time and with lots of conversation, they both adjusted to their new lives. At some point, she says, "You finally just get it, and then, that all ends."

Of course, not everyone has a child who heads off to college or moves away from home after high school. Some kids choose a different path, and some are not able to attend school for a host of reasons from finances to illness to physical and/or learning disabilities. For Sara Parriott, mom of two and television writer and producer, it took some time to find the right place for her son, who has developmental delays. "It was a big struggle," she says. The ultimate goal was to help him live in a setting that gave him a sense of independence and gave them confidence in his care.

When the reality that your eighteen years of active parenting are up, take a breath and Dr. Hartstein's advice: "Remind yourself of all the things you've done to prepare your teen for this big day and that it is part of life and needs to happen. Although it may feel sad, it's important that your child move into the world." What kids need now is not instructions about how to do everything right but the resourcefulness and resilience to cope with things when they go wrong. And that includes having parents to call on when they need advice.

I wrote to my youngest son when he left for school. It seemed more natural to our relationship than trying to say it all as we parted ways. And yes, I did offer some advice, though it was nothing he hadn't heard before. I wanted to remind him of his worth, his talents, that perfection is not the goal—the journey is—and that no matter what, I'd be here for him.

⌒

Wait just a minute.

You don't like it when I'm sentimental, but how can I not be today? You're heading off to college, and there are a few things I've got to say.

You were born an original and inspired me to see the world anew. Not through the prism of pink that I had known, but through the eyes of a boy who delighted in stories about superheroes and tales of the impossible. A boy who found beauty in bugs and things that go bump in the night; a boy who swung from the limbs of a tree and made magic swords from the branches it dropped and slew dragons and monsters and bad guys.

You're a boy after my own heart.

There's no one more fun to share a meal with or more willing to help make homemade biscuits at midnight, then devour them with apricot jam.

And when you got sick that cruel year, it was me who got mad at the world, not you. Then, just when it seemed the illness would never end, it did...though admittedly, we were never quite the same. Now there's a shadow that lurks behind us.

Movies are your future. You told me so when you were nine years old. And now here we are, packing up your suitcases so you can go away and learn how to make them the way you dream them.

While you're away, be the friend you'd like to have. Go on adventures, but promise you'll pause first to consider the what-ifs. Be spontaneous, but believe me when I say that some things cannot be undone. Choices are exactly that—choices—and dares are designed by bullies, not friends.

We tried to instill the right values in you. Hone them, and value your impact on others and the world at large. What do you stand for? Actions have repercussions, and people will judge you less sympathetically now that you're on your own.

Don't expect to do everything right, right from the start. Anyone who has ever accomplished anything made mistakes—but they learned from them. Learning is a process, and this is your time to ask questions and seek answers, to make the most of the gifts you've been given and the opportunities you've been granted.

The clothes you laid out are ready to go. I added a few things—more hats and gloves for the winter, and an extra blanket. Linens and towels, Band-Aids and balms. Your favorite books and comics. All pieces of your home for your new home.

There's one more thing: take my love with you.

Long after I'm gone, it will be there for you.

~

He was a magical kid. Right from the start. The first few hours after he was born, he was too weak to nurse, so the specialist fed him from a tube. Like Popeye downing a can of spinach, my youngest son inhaled the formula and gained instant strength. By the time he was done, his eyes had opened, met mine, and cast their spell—a spell I've been under ever since. It wouldn't be the last time he had a Popeye response to food, especially in the morning...

~

Thank goodness for whoever invented breakfast. Without it, there's no telling when Nick might voluntarily converse. By his senior year in high school, I could count on the fingers of one hand the number of actual conversations we'd had before he'd eaten something. Speaking of eating, boy, can he. I once got a call from a mom during a sleepover asking if it was okay to give him more than the ten slices of bacon and several servings of eggs he had just consumed. She'd never seen anything like it: he was as light as a feather—where did it go? At the Air and Space Museum cafeteria in DC when he was five years old, he asked for a second foot-long hot dog. When we explained it was more hot dog than could literally fit into his stomach, he started to cry. I had to look away from those baby blues to offer him an apple instead.

Thirteen years later, we were at his college fifteen hundred miles from home, settling him in for his freshman year. After all the packing and unpacking, scrubbing, organizing, bed-making, suitemate and suitemate-parent introductions, it was time for my husband and me to take our leave. I was fairly seasoned at this routine, having settled our oldest into his college dorm twice before. The difference was my family lived an hour away from his school, and I knew they'd be there if he needed them, even if just for a good meal. But this time, there was no family nearby, no one to say to this kid, "Come for dinner." So I was gearing up to do what no new mother thinks she will ever do—walk away (fly away, actually) and leave her child.

How would he get by without a kitchen? How would he fuel his creativity to become the filmmaker he's been saying he wants to be since he was a single digit? And just as important, how could he fit anything besides two tiny water bottles and two ice cubes in the mini-fridge that he shared with his roommate?

Clearly, I had food on my mind, and there are so many Nick food memories. Once, when he was just starting to crawl, he paused to have a snack of Cheerios. When he was done, instead of resuming the crawling, he simply rolled across the floor, giggling as if he had discovered the newest, greatest means of transportation. At the age of one, while in his high chair, he fell asleep eating noodles. When I went to pick him up, he opened his eyes and yelled "More!" As a newly minted teen, after a night of watching reruns of *Diners, Drive-ins, and Dives,* we both got so hungry, he suggested we head out for groceries at 11:00 p.m. so we could cook up some of what we saw on TV. And we did.

Of course, I knew he wouldn't actually starve in college. As required by the school, he did have a meal plan. And as required by me, he had half the snacks from the local Target store packed in plastic tubs and jammed into his too-small closet: peanut butter, power bars, ramen, nuts, and tuna packets (which, I suspect, once opened in a small space, could give a freshman a reputation he might not wish for).

Still, how could I leave him? How could I walk away from this boy who had brought me so much joy, whom I nurtured a little less every year as he began the shift to living away, but whom I loved even more than I thought possible?

I handed him the coin I'd gotten for the occasion—the one with the lucky clover—and told him to keep it with him always. To pull it out if he was feeling like things weren't going his way, or if he needed a reminder that he is always in my heart. (And I reminded him of the importance of staying ahead of the hunger.) That's when our eyes met, and in spite of the approaching dinner hour, I saw the sparkle in his.

He was going to be fine.

Still, a week after I returned home, just in case, I sent him a care package anyway.

⌒

After I dropped him off at college, I was determined to be okay, but I knew it would take more than talk. It would take action, which I soon discovered was not so simple. Especially because we suddenly had so many empty couches.

PART TWO

WALLOWING IN THE PAST
AND ON THE COUCH

The Initial Shock

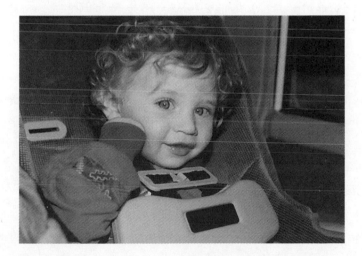

T he minute I walked in the door, I felt his absence…

This is about a room. No. It's about a boy.

When he went to sleep that night nine years ago, our first night in this house, boxes were piled high around him. Before he fell asleep, I read to him from his favorite book, *The Stinky Cheese Man and Other Fairly Stupid Tales*—I'd packed it along with his teddy bear and his new blue-and-green comforter and marked the box "open first."

After the story, I lay next to him for a while, the lights still on. He wasn't ready, he said, to turn them off or for me to go. So I pushed the hidden button on the teddy bear's heart, the one that triggered the thirty-second recording of me singing a few lines from "Help!" It had become his lullaby when he was an infant, when I was so sleep-deprived that I couldn't remember the words to any other song. *God help me*, I thought at the time, *I've lost my memory*, but then the lyrics came pouring out.

I watched him as he grew sleepy. His skin was flawless, his curls soft and long. I knew he was halfway between the years of wide-eyed wonder and those of surly rebellion—the time of bliss—and I wanted to savor every moment. *What a boy*, I thought. *What a magical nine-year-old boy.* When he laughed, it made me laugh. When he cried, it made my heart ache. If he were selling dirt door-to-door and I'd never met him and didn't need any dirt, just one look at that face, and I'd have bought a truckload.

We sang along, and he pushed the button over and over until he drifted off. And when he was really asleep (not just opening one eye to see if I was still there), I got to work.

I had made up my mind that I was going to unpack all the boxes in his room, so that when he opened his eyes the next morning, he'd find it entirely different from when he closed them.

The six months leading up to the thirteen-hundred-mile move from Maryland had been hard: his father had gone ahead of us for his job, while we stayed behind to finish the school year. That winter was brutal, one of the worst in memory—one ice storm after another, followed by difficult good-byes to friends, to teachers, to the home and the places he loved. Now, here we were in an unfamiliar place, and I wanted to make him happy, wanted to give back some of the bliss he'd given me, just by being him. So I set to work on creating a space that he would enjoy the way he had his old room, where he acted out characters from books, making tinfoil swords to save creatures large and small and marching toy soldiers across the floor.

Fortunately, he slept like a log. I hung clothes in his closet and capes and hats on wooden pegs, put books on shelves, pictures on the walls, toys in drawers and buckets. I displayed the LEGOs he'd built, filled a basket with his toy swords, put trading cards on his desk, and lay his moon-and-stars rug on the floor. Over his bed, I hung the yellow Styrofoam sun with a smiling face.

At 4:00 a.m., I was done. I'd even flattened the boxes and carried them to our box-filled garage. Before I went to sleep, I set my alarm for 8:00 a.m.—I wanted to see the expression on his face when he woke up.

At 7:00 a.m., he was standing next to my bed.

"Mom," he said, touching my arm. "Mom, wake up, please."

"Why are you awake so early?" I asked, sitting up.

"'Cause something happened when I was sleeping," he said.

"What?" I asked.

"My room got nice. The boxes are gone," he said. "You gotta come see my room."

Last week, after taking him to college, I packed up that same room. Some of his things will be given away, some thrown away, some kept for memory's sake. He still had the swords and the trading cards, but most of the other things had been replaced over the years. I found a Target gift card with $7.42 left on it and used it to buy him something he'd forgotten to take to school. There were a few drawings and pictures left on the wall—he'd mailed his favorite posters to his dorm, including several of the Beatles. His closet was mostly empty, save for a few hanging items wrapped in plastic: the wool blazer my mother gave him when he was a toddler, the band shirts, the honor society tees, the tiny fake leather jacket he wore when he pretended to be Elvis.

I vacuumed curtains, walls, and dried-up toothpaste on the carpet.

I dusted the sun with the smiling face.

The button on the bear had long ago lost its juice, but I sat down on his bed and sang the lullaby one last time.

"Help me if you can, I'm feeling down..."

⌒

My boys were gone. Unless you count Benjamin, who didn't have a room, only a doggie bed now flush against my side of the bed I share with my husband. No doubt Benjamin was feeling their absence as well. He was in search of his pack. Perhaps anticipating the emotional toll that the task of cleaning Nick's room would take, I decided on the flight home not to attempt it for several days. Actually, as it turned out, I couldn't. And that solved that.

⌒

Within hours of returning home from taking our youngest son to college, I was sick. The kind of fever, chills, sore-throat sick that I hadn't experienced in years. We'd had a whirlwind week of packing, commuting, cleaning, and moving. In Brooklyn, at the only Target in town, every parent and student from miles around appeared to be stocking up for the year. People were literally grabbing things off shelves before someone else grabbed them first. It was an all-out school supply war in a city not known for personal space, and I figured it was only a matter of time before I picked up somebody's crud. Or before it all just caught up with me.

The only upside to my illness was that I was mostly stuck in bed, which meant I didn't venture into the kids' bedrooms. This, in turn, delayed my experiencing a completely childless home—at least from a visual standpoint.

In the days that followed our return, in addition to suppressing my sneezing with antihistamines, I had to suppress the desire to call or text Nick.

My husband and I were checking with each other constantly to see if our son had communicated something...anything. Me: "Did you hear anything?" Him: "No, you?"

I knew from experience that making the shift to being the parent of a young adult who no longer lives in the same house takes some practice. You can't ask them about their day, every day—about whom they met, what they learned, if they liked the movie they saw or the book they read—and it hits hard. You go from mostly knowing where they are and what they're doing and who they're doing it with to...zilch. The first week, you go through withdrawal. It's like having had chocolate every day of your life, your entire life, and then not being able to have the tiniest taste. And you really love chocolate.

But they do communicate eventually, and much like learning to interpret a newborn's cries, you learn to read their moods based on their method of communication. Phone calls are for expressing extremes such as happiness or sadness, though occasionally, they can be used for describing something so detailed it's just plain easier to say it on the phone. Emails are for forwarding other emails that are usually about money or for giving a heads-up about something that occurs to them at 3:00 in the morning. Texts are for laundry questions and HAHA-type things—which I must admit, I began to enjoy once I realized that HAHA does not mean someone is being sarcastic but is actually smiling or laughing (and cooler than the LOL I had only just recently gotten used to).

When Alex first went away to college, I tried to ease the transition by sending him occasional text messages and pictures of our dog, Benjamin. Sometimes I put a hat on him. Sometimes he was just Benjamin doing what he does best—sleeping or playing with his toys. Fortunately, the dog is wonderfully compliant, though he often looks at me as if to say, "Seriously?" And sometimes he "disses" me—looks away just when I snap the picture. And the photos of him doing this—doing anything, really—always inspire a HAHA reply from my son, so much so that if I haven't sent a photo of Benjamin in a while, he'll ask for one.

Of course, I know what his request for pictures of Benjamin mean, just as he knows what I mean when I send them. And that's the beauty of it—nary a word has to be said.

Up until last week when he left for his freshman year at college, Nick only texted me when he was going to be late for dinner, needed ten dollars, or forgot something at school. But two days after taking him to college—and pacing the floor a few million times, waiting for something, anything—I received this text message:

"Mom, when you have time today, can you text me a picture of Benjamin?"

I sent him several.

~

J. D. Rothman is a mom of two. She writes for television and film (*Angelina Ballerina, Arthur, The Trumpet of the Swan*, and more) and is a children's media producer, lyricist, and author. Rothman traveled to India with her husband immediately after her second son left for school. The goal was to avoid thinking about how empty the house would be when she returned. "If I could have, I would have stayed for four months," she told me. But return she did, and when she did, she began worrying about whether she had done everything she should have to prepare her kids for life. Her worries and those of other parents became the basis for her humorous blog (http://theneuroticpar-ent.com/), which she began anonymously while on an eight-state, twelve-college tour with her oldest son. Her strategy of avoidance made sense to me until I read about what therapists think about it, and even then, it still made sense to me until I heard from friends that it hits you in some way, regardless. Humor helps. Seriously. Here's a post written after she dropped her son off at school:

THE KIDS ARE ALL RIGHT...
BUT THE PARENTS ARE NOT

It's fall, and the moms of new college students are not doing well. Many aren't sleeping. One stayed in bed for several days eating tapioca. Others spend most of their time discussing their fears about mono with their Pilates instructors. But the smart ones got right on a plane after move-in and headed to Tuscany.

Most dads are deeply invested in their midlife crises. Lots of surfing, biking, tennis, flying lessons, brocations to Buenos Aires, and purchasing expensive BBQ equipment.

Boys, especially those related to me, are hopeless at communication. They will answer texts, usually within thirty-six hours, but mostly with one-word mispellllled responses with extra letters for emphasis. Occasionally they say they are tired, specifically the day after tailgates. Frustratingly, they have been rumored to have participated in lengthy iChats with their high school friends.

The majority of girls are in heaven, texting liiiike thisss by October, but complain nonstop the first two weeks about:

- too much reading
- art history is not challenging enough
- messy roommate
- partying roommate
- food not as good as when they toured the school
- dorm room too hot
- shower too cold
- missing their friends

Parents of older kids confirm over and over again that no news is good news. Three report that the only time they heard from their sons and daughters during freshman year was when they spilled coffee on their laptops or they were in police custody.

A lot of women choose not to deal with the idea of their child moving out until the day comes. And even after the move, they busy themselves with all kinds of things to avoid being home. Then the rains come. Literally and figuratively. When they're forced to be at home, often because of something as simple as the weather, they lose it. I asked Dr. Hartstein about this practice of avoidance. "If you act as if it's no big deal," she says, "this could trickle down to your child's denial, which isn't helpful either. Denial in general isn't the greatest coping strategy. It prevents problem solving and attention to the change that is inevitable. If you talk openly about what's happening, the whole family will be better prepared."

I was prepared. Totally. But it still hit me and hit me hard. It's like being in a theater that has gone totally dark. Half my house was empty and still. My husband, a man who is fond of routines, couldn't seem to find a rhythm. The dog wandered from room to room, seeking and not finding. I think we were all sort of in shock. And yes, I've read about the "Boomerang Generation"—young adults who return to live with their parents—and how it's changed the empty nest. Recent census data show that as many as twenty-two million eighteen- to thirty-four-year-olds (31 percent of that age group) were living at home with their parents—more than double the number two decades ago. People love to remind *almost* and *new* empty nesters of this fact. But if your child heads off to school or to live away from home, having someone say this to you only discounts what may very well feel like a profound loss or ending. And that's because it is—you will no longer be under one roof, where traditions were born, memories made, lives built. Once the kids leave, it's never the same. And no, that's not a bad thing. But it is a different thing.

If someone breaks their leg, you don't tell them with a wave of your hand that it's nothing, that they'll be healed in three months. You acknowledge their pain, both emotional and physical. They still have to live through the process—see and feel their leg every day and adapt to the resulting changes their injury put in motion.

The same thing goes for a parent whose child has just left home: their pain is real, and they need time.

After the college trip, while I was sick and trying to figure out how to use the TV remote, I thought about all the years I'd spent parenting—what I did best, what I could have done better, and what I had forgotten to tell my children. Had I prepared them properly for life? Would they make friends who understood and respected them the way they deserved to be understood and respected? Would anyone try to harm them? Would they remember what to do if *they* got sick or where the thermometer was? When both the kids left, it really did feel as if there had been some kind of a death in the family. I could hardly stand the lack of energy in the house. Running away (temporarily) to someplace else sounded good at first, until I remembered I had no place to run to and all my money was tied up in putting my kids through college. Moving someplace new might have worked—you know, new home, new vibe—but I wasn't ready for that transition. Not yet, anyway. I just couldn't figure out how to leave a past that I'd loved so much.

"You are grieving," psychologist Margaret Rutherford told me. "It's not that you aren't, but you have to learn to refocus on the positive."

I did. I said things like: *The positive is that my kids made it to college. The positive is that I like my kids and they like me (most of the time). The positive is that my kids are kind. And they have goals. And know how to stretch a dollar.*

But mostly, I was positive that I was still bummed.

~

Of all the changes we feel when the kids leave home, the change in routine is probably the most impactful. Anyone who's ever returned to a home that is missing someone knows that memories are around every corner, and for better or worse, they're hard to ignore. In his book *The Examined Life*, Dr. Stephen Grosz points out that loss and change are "deeply connected—there cannot be change without loss." *New York Times* columnist Charles M. Blow, in his essay "The Passion of Parenting," captured these sentiments precisely:

> I thought that this would be a celebratory time, a time when I would relish the idea of getting back to me, of working late without worry and taking last-minute weekend jaunts.
>
> But I don't. Letting go is hard for me to do. I must let go, but my heart feels hollow. I can't imagine me without them.

Winifred White Neisser, mom of two and a former television executive with NBC and Sony, says, "Once the kids are in the house, you can barely remember what life was like before they were there." This makes it difficult to comprehend what it will be like after they leave, and you begin to imagine all sorts of scenarios. She was particularly nervous about how quiet it would be when her oldest—her daughter, who was always so upbeat—was headed for school: "Before they left, I was worried there would be this huge hole." By the time her son left two years later, she realized there wasn't a hole at all. Neisser remained very much connected to them, and though her son and daughter had very different approaches to staying in touch with her, they developed a rhythm.

A friend told her a story about a single parent and how she

described the first few weeks after her child went to college: "The first week, I walked around the house crying. The second week, I walked around the house lost. And the third week, I walked around the house naked." Neisser laughed when she heard this but related on some level: "When both kids left, there was a certain freedom and reclaiming of the territory that I guess I didn't realize I'd lost. It's very much a mixed bag. I miss them, and when they come home, I'm always really happy to see them, and the house feels full again. And then, when they leave, I'm sort of glad to have the house to myself." Her best advice to moms who are about to go through the transition? It was something her husband said to her, actually: "It's the normal process of things, and you just have to sort of let it happen." Sounds almost too obvious, I know, but it's reassuring if you think about it. When Neisser was a teenager and leaving for school, she never considered how her own parents felt—she just took it for granted that they would be fine. In retrospect, she wonders how it impacted them and wishes they were still around to ask. One thing she does know is that they never laid a guilt trip on her about leaving or said they'd prefer she stayed closer to home, as most of her friends did. And this strikes her now as a gift. "You have to give kids the freedom to go out and be who they are," she says.

If I Knew Then…

It really is true that with time comes clarity. Perhaps it's due to the physical distance—when you're not physically around your kids and caught up in the moments, the days, the years, you're able to be somewhat less emotional and tap into your inner Spock. Or Spockmom, as the case may be.

If I could do it all again—raise a family—I would in an instant. But I'd do it a little differently, because hindsight, it turns out, really is 20/20. I realized this not long after my kids left, when I had the chance to focus on myself, to reflect upon the ways parenting had changed me and the things I learned. I think you can only really accomplish this properly when you've achieved some distance from the role. I'd raise my family differently, not because of the mistakes I made—though I certainly made my share—but because time means so much more to me now. I understand it better and its importance...and the way parents use it, lose track of it, and wish it away or wish for more. It's all about the time we spend together as a family, the time parents spend making decisions and avoiding decisions; doing the right thing and the wrong thing; and consoling, teaching, reading, talking, dancing, playing, working, dreaming, laughing. It all comes down to time.

If I had the time to do it all again, I'd:

1. Give myself permission to not be on call 24/7. By permission, I don't mean disappearing without a trace or for long, drawn-out periods. But I do mean handing over the reins of parenting more often so I keep in touch with who I am in addition to being a parent.

2. Enjoy a regular date night with my husband at least twice a month. Away from home if possible, but if we can't, at least pretend we are.

3. Let the laundry pile up. Because, let's be honest, nobody is going to fire me.

4. Swing on the swings with the kids. Fun is more fun when your mother is having it too.

5. Make fewer to-do lists. They only beget more to-do lists, and

though I might feel as if I'm accomplishing something, I'm only writing down what I already know.

6. Have more "backward days," where dinner is for breakfast and breakfast is for dinner.

7. Sleep more, better, longer.

8. Worry less, better, shorter.

9. Take time for tea. The entire process of making and drinking it—slowly—is an art. Zen. Brilliant.

10. Be less grumpy about the state of my kids' rooms. They'll be empty far too soon.

11. Dance. Regardless of how dumb or goofy I look doing it. Knees don't stay young forever.

12. Write down the bedtime stories I make up for my kids. And even better, the ones they make up for me. We don't think so at the moment, but memory fades. The written word lives on.

13. Step out of my comfort zone more often. I'm a role model, after all, for making dreams come true.

14. Be less polite to people who are unpleasant. I'm not going to change them.

15. Drink more milk. Strong bones mean I can lift my kids and run with them—and one day, with their kids.

16. Knit. Somebody always needs a sweater, blanket, scarf, hat, mittens, or socks. Plus, it's strangely soothing.

17. Travel more. Regardless of the obstacles. It's an education in itself.

18. Repeat number 8.

Introspection at this point in life is right on cue, especially an analysis of our own parenting skills. It makes sense if you think about it—we've stepped back to take a new look at the child we've nearly raised, because he or she is entering the adult world. The goal is to say and do the right things, teach them the big lessons, and we often end up using our own upbringing as a guide. Dr. Pickhardt says that how we are treated by our parents affects how we are "internally scripted" and how we end up treating our kids. "By their parental example, interaction, and instruction, we are taught how to parent: but we only access this learning when we have children of our own," he says. "We are always working off of the two models our parents gave—how to be and how not to be." He calls it revisionist parenting. Compensation and overcompensation is part of it. Pickhardt says revisionist parents make up for how they were treated by treating their children differently. Sometimes this is good, and sometimes not so much.

As we go through this process of preparing our kids for their own lives and weighing our role, both past and future, Pickhardt stresses that it's important to understand that "the outcome of parenting doesn't just depend on the individual parent, but also on the child."

I do wish I'd read this excerpt from his *Psychology Today* blog when I was a young mom forging my own path:

Just be gentle as you work to free yourself from following old lessons that were given many years ago, internalized when you were too young to know the patterns you were learning. Consider invoking that mantra from Alcoholics Anonymous: "Progress, not perfection." Accept that there will be slips along the way, incidents of backsliding or overreactions you wish did not occur. Since they are now exceptions in your conduct, not the rule, they provide evidence that you are gradually succeeding in accomplishing the revision you desire. Now repeat to yourself, *I am not my parent, I am my own person, and I can choose to function my independent way.*

In hindsight, when my mother came to spend the holidays with us the winter before our youngest left for school, I didn't fully understand *why* I felt like I did. Yes, I was thrilled to share it with her, to be able to give her things and gain a better sense of intimacy. But it turns out that much of what was so emotional for me was the realization that she and I were in fact finally growing closer, simultaneous to my letting go of my own children. And it had taken a really long time to get here. Our relationship, just like my relationship with my kids, was entering a new phase and needed to be redefined. Of course, some of it could have been that I just wanted my mother. Pickhardt says that most of us don't ever "outgrow" that want, even if we don't say it out loud.

My mother was the product of an era when moms shared little about their own lives and asked little about what was personal to you. Essentially, feelings were swept under the rug. Without intimacy or sharing personal information about yourself, experts say it can be especially daunting for adolescents to communicate what's on their mind for fear of being judged or made to feel inadequate or incompetent. I wanted something much more intimate with my own kids and didn't want them to have to wait until I was a grandmother to achieve it.

After my children left for school, I found myself observing from a distance the community I once felt so much a part of—families with young children. I thought about what great parents we'd all be if we could download each other's learned parenting knowledge and share it with one another. Since that's science fiction, I asked some moms if there was anything they would have done differently in the years leading up to their kids going to school, just as I had. Again, not regrets but approaches they might have tried because of lessons they learned along the way. I was surprised to find the word "wish" come up repeatedly. Lisa Carpenter, who blogs at www.grandmasbriefs.com, reflects on the high school years while her kids were still at home:

> I wish I had spent more time enjoying my daughters in those final years before they left for college, rather than continually coming down hard on them, ensuring they were following the steps required for their future. So much of my time was spent demanding they do this or that, fill out the right forms, master the right tests, talk to the right people, meet deadlines, and make decisions. It was so stressful for both sides and created a black cloud of tension and animosity...and guilt and sadness on my part once the child was out the door. Occasional "time out" sessions of one-on-one dinners together or outings in which we just appreciated one another without focusing on the college prep to-do list would have made the transition and our final years together more enjoyable.

J. D. Rothman says it's more about what she didn't do, perhaps, that she thinks about most. "I wish I had ingrained in them to stay in better touch with me. *I can't talk now—love you*, has become their bittersweet mantra."

Journalist Jane Pauley struggled with finding just the right balance between mother and advisor: "I wasn't a helicopter parent, but my family won't let me deny I'm prone to heavy advice giving. And yet I remember overhearing a roommate in deep discussion with his mom about his course selection and thinking, *way too involved!* I let the kids find their way, but I think I expected the college would take care that 'exploring' wouldn't become 'squandering.' I was more assertive about getting them to spend time with academic advisors, though I wish I could say I'd been more successful."

At this point, you may also be thinking about missed opportunities in work or love—regretting choices you made under the influence of youthful optimism and naïveté. It happens to all of us. My mother told me recently that she has many regrets, mostly about the career she didn't have because she had no role models, no mentors to urge her on. In this stage of life, we're rich in wisdom—richer than we may realize—and we have what it takes to mentor ourselves. But if we wallow in regret, it can be paralyzing. Reflection (the right kind of reflection) can help us grow; regret, not so much. Here's Dr. Margaret Rutherford's take on it:

When approaching a child's departure from the home, I frequently hear regret. Things as simple as "I wish I had gone to more of her games" and "I feel bad because I didn't cook," to more serious considerations: "I should have talked less and listened more; gotten divorced; stayed married; stopped drinking; made him get a job."

Regret reflects a sense of responsibility, and that's an honorable thing. But when it is taken too far, it can keep you stuck in the past, concentrating on something you are powerless to change. That can lead to worse things. Shame.

Self-loathing. Despair. Depression. When you look up the definition of regret, it includes words like "to mourn" and "have remorse." Healthy regret moves through stages, as in grief. The operable word there is *moves*. If you do have regret, then it can be recognized. To be healthy, it shouldn't crystallize into something immovable.

Reflection is a different animal. It suggests making sure your brain is attached as you filter through the past so that you don't get bogged down in any emotion. It is a more cerebral event. It's not necessarily superior to experiencing regret. Both processes have their place. Regret is not a bad thing, unless it remains stagnant. Stationary. If you recognize it, and it leads to a change in your future choices, it can help you create a life—a relationship—where you feel better.

Whatever mistakes or regrets you have, admit them. Say you are sorry, and move on. Everyone has made a mistake or two. Or more. Continue your life as a mom—as an individual who puts both feet on the floor every morning and is trying to live and love well.

⌣

We come in all shapes and sizes, all manner of opinion, tradition, and circumstance. We are not born mothers, regardless of what our children may think. Our knowledge does not arrive in a neat little box with a satin bow. We learn by watching others, through sheer will, strength, and adversity. We are on the front lines. Some of us hover, and some parent from afar. No matter what our style, we are questioned, challenged, revered, reviled. And, fortunately, loved—though never quite as much as we love.

We are mothers.

We are single, married, divorced, gay, straight. We are perfect; we are imperfect; we are tough; we are soft; we keep therapists in business. We are doctors without licenses, perpetually on call to remedy ills and fix broken hearts.

We are cheering squads, disciplinarians, realists, dreamers, playmates, chefs, and detectives. We are students of life, professors of whatever the day brings.

Whether we work at home or in an office, our job description is long and our days are too short. Whether we have money to burn or none to spare, our salary is the same. It won't buy what's in any store, but it can make us feel richer just the same.

We are mothers.

Most of us do it for love, a few for glory, and some just do it. All of us have the power to change lives.

We are nearly 90 million strong and sisters at heart. Still, sometimes we are each other's toughest critics and forget we have one another to fall back on. We are our own best source of inspiration, courage, advice, and kindness.

We are mothers.

When the earliest memories of our children begin to fade—memories of their first steps, first words, first day of school—we work to keep them alive. We make scrapbooks, take photos, carry images in our hearts.

We are mothers.

There are those of us who believe that mistakes cannot be guarded against, that the old ways are the best. Others say history is to be learned from but should not be repeated, that the future must be written anew.

One day soon, when some of us least expect it, the future will arrive. Our kids will be grown, and we'll move on with our lives separate from theirs. And when it does, and we are in the company of women friends both old and new, we'll be reminded not of our differences but of the single most important way we are the same.

We are mothers.

~

The Hardest Part

My son's leaving for college was complicated by, well, complications.

~

On a beautiful October afternoon in 2007, my bright-eyed twelve-year-old son, Nicholas, my youngest, went for a bike ride and returned fifteen minutes later with a lackluster gaze and the feeling he was on a boat in the high seas. That moment began a medical mystery that rocked our family's world and changed him in more ways than one. A day after Nick's dizziness started, fatigue set in. Swollen glands followed close behind. Our general practitioner ordered blood work, including tests for mononucleosis and Lyme disease. When everything came back negative, we tried steroids for his swollen glands and a round of antibiotics in case he had a bacterial infection. When the dizziness and fatigue persisted, we wondered aloud if the culprit might have been the flu shot he received eight days prior. It was presumed he had viral labyrinthitis (an inner-ear disorder) that would pass in a week or two.

When it didn't, and his tonsils grew exponentially, we tried a different antibiotic. All the while, he was perched in a makeshift bed on our first floor—an overstuffed chair and aging ottoman with a twin sheet stretched to its limit. Suffering from extreme vertigo, Nick was unable to walk up the stairs to his bedroom. He could not lift his head without looking as if he were drowning, and mostly, he slept the days away. School became someplace his friends went.

After several weeks, I went into investigative mode and searched for an ear, nose, and throat (ENT) specialist. It took a month to get an appointment. "Is he a patient?" I was asked repeatedly. Once there, more tests were ordered. One doc said they revealed an issue with his mastoid (a portion of the temporal bone). The ENT disagreed. He said that Nick's right inner ear was damaged, but he couldn't really say why. All he told me was that he doubted he could fix it. Ever.

That's not what a mother wants to hear.

The ENT referred us to a neurotologist (a combination neurologist and ENT), and we were given an "urgent appointment," which really meant waiting several more weeks. The original ENT assured me that he had personally spoken with this new doctor about Nick's case.

When we finally met with the specialist, he hadn't a clue who Nick was. The visit went downhill from there. He spoke in monosyllables, answering our questions in the barest of terms. He said Nick simply had viral labyrinthitis and that the condition would clear up in a few weeks. But just in case, to see if there was something more than a virus causing Nick's condition, he ordered "vestibular" testing, which entailed body harnesses, floors that dip, goggles with cameras, and chairs that spin. In the end, they only proved what we already knew—Nick was dizzy—but showed no underlying cause. The same inner-ear test the original ENT ordered was also repeated, and it showed no damage—the opposite of what the first round of tests had shown.

We began to push for physical rehab to help Nick walk. When months went by—the ENT clearly uninterested, never following up, in spite of the fact he had written an open-ended note to Nick's school that he was under his care and unable to attend—we sought out a neurologist. He suggested salt pills, mentioning something about fluid retention and blood pressure. After calling eight different pharmacies, I finally learned they no longer existed.

By February, Nick looked so dreadful, he was hospitalized. We spent seven days there, Nick in his hospital bed and me sleeping on the chair next to him. At the hospital, Nick had more tests to rule out the bad stuff. Fortunately, those tests came back negative, but unfortunately, the doctors still couldn't give us an answer. All they could say was that yes, something was wrong, but they weren't sure whether the problem was with Nick's ear or whether it was neurological.

By May, I'd taken matters into my own hands, and we were on our way to the Mayo Clinic in Minnesota. Instead of relying on doctors who didn't collaborate and wouldn't refute each other's ideas, I'd written my own report and sent it to Mayo, asking if they would see him, and to my insurance company to try and get approvals for the clinic. The process took around two months but paid off. The team of doctors there put Nick through a slew of tests. Some were new, some repeat, and all the results were shared between them in real time, discussed with kindness and understanding and without a clock to guide them.

In the end, they said Nick's dizziness stemmed from serious inner-ear damage caused by a virus of some sort, perhaps exacerbated by the flu shot, but that it could be reversed over time with intensive physical therapy that focused on balance. He was lucky, they said, that he had not lost his hearing. Though the doctors said it would likely be another six months or longer before the dizziness waned, with a diagnosis and exercises to do at home, Nick finally had a goal—and hope.

When we returned to Texas, we lined the upstairs hallway with blue painter's tape laid out in rows and boxes. He followed the rows like a game of hopscotch without the hop—attempting to keep his feet in the boxes until he got to the last box and turned around to do it again. Sometimes he sang the *Rocky* score when he got to the end. Sometimes I did too.

Nick recovered gradually. Since he couldn't attend school during the year he was sick, a special teacher from the county school system came to him several days a week. She sat next to him as he lay on the couch, finding inventive ways to keep him learning and engaged. After one year away from school, he finally returned, a changed young man. He still has some lasting effects, though if you didn't know him well, you wouldn't notice; he has adapted and learned to do what he needs to in order to thrive. He's my Rocky, after all.

⌇

I've read stories about people who literally fall off a horse, suffer all kinds of physical and emotional trauma, and then, as soon as they've healed, climb right back on. After he recovered, I encouraged Nick to do the equivalent. But I found myself on a sort of low-level alert, constantly looking for any sign that his illness had returned so I could stop it before it took hold. I was the night watchman: even when he was in the hospital, I would try to stay up each night as long as I could to make sure, you know, that he was breathing. I had lost faith in the medical system, and the only people I could rely on were a couple of family members, my husband, and me.

As I struggled to get past this stage of the transition, the word *vulnerability* came up repeatedly. I felt vulnerable because I was scared. Scared for my children, scared about my future, and of the unknown in general. It's no secret to anyone who knows me that I like to be in control. If I'm in control, I can predict outcomes, set a course, see results. Or so I thought. How can I find that sense of control again, of setting a course and proceeding with it?

I'm smarter than I was twenty years ago. I understand the way the world works—what is expected of me, what I expect of myself. But smart is irrelevant when approaching an entirely new stage of life. New requires a willingness to take chances and permission to fail. Which brings me back to the topic of vulnerability and Dr. Brené Brown. In her popular 2010 Ted Talk, Brown says that through research, she discovered, much to her surprise, that courage is borne out of vulnerability. One of the things courageous people have in common is that they "fully embrace vulnerability." In fact, they readily do things where the outcome is not certain. She also found that people with a strong sense of love and belonging have that sense because they feel worthy of it. It all got me thinking about moms in transition: the courage, the vulnerability, the sense of worthiness. That maybe, somewhere along the way, we lose ourselves a little in our role as a mother, and when we do, we also lose sight of our sense of worthiness. Or perhaps some of us never fully realized it before we took on our roles as mothers, and it comes back later to bite us in the rear.

The Importance of Shifting the Focus to You

Do children come first in your family? Do their needs take precedence over your mate's? Most of the women I interviewed for this book said they do. You might be surprised to learn that therapists advise against this. "The mental health community believes family should be couple-centered rather than kid-centered," says psychologist and parenting and teen expert Dr. Barbara Greenberg. One of the risks of being kid-centered is that it can make it difficult for couples to stay connected.

That overwhelming sense that kids come first for many moms is, in fact, very "primal," says Greenberg, an author and mom who admits that she too put her daughter first: "Even women who are working full-time—their kids are often number one. Their secondary role is that of worker/partner/friend." She suggests you redefine your roles before the kids leave the nest. If you define yourself as a mother first, it's very difficult to fully define yourself, especially when the kids leave home.

Josann McGibbon, a divorced mom of two and a writer for film and television including the hit shows *Desperate Housewives* and *The Starter Wife*, along with the movie *Runaway Bride*, says her kids have always come first. After McGibbon's oldest daughter left for college, she rearranged dining-room table seating, changed her routine, etc., but she couldn't shake the feeling that life as she knew it was over. *I'll never be part of her daily life again*, she thought. Within a month, things had improved. "She was so happy…her happiness made it a happy thing."

Mary Dell Harrington, cofounder of the popular blog Grown and Flown (http://grownandflown.com/) and mom of two, believes that children's needs come first for a very long time in a family's life. "As parents," she says, "our job is to provide for our kids until they are able to take on the responsibilities for themselves."

When you've spent eighteen years focused on raising children—putting their needs first—it can be tricky getting into the habit of refocusing on yourself.

It's not uncommon to get excited thinking about all the

possibilities of a new future, then become overwhelmed with the reality that there is a lot to do and suddenly stop and say, *never mind*. It's that whole notion of loss of control/vulnerability again.

Risa Nye, a mom of three, journalist, and blogger (http://www .risanye.com/), puts it this way:

> When kids leave home, it's more often than not a bitter-sweet experience. It means that one stage is ending and another beginning for you as a parent. It might be scary, it might mean you have to come to terms with your own next chapter, and it may mean some very big changes in other parts of your life. I was not an overly involved parent, yet I still felt those twinges when my three left one at a time over the course of eight years. Being sad and depressed when change occurs may just be your normal pattern of reacting to it. In my situation, the first one to leave was my daughter. I probably felt the saddest when she left because she was going far away from home. By the time my youngest left, I had a better idea of how long "the blues" would last and could figure I'd get over it in time. I wouldn't call the feelings I had true depression—just a sadness that lasted a little while.

At this point, I'd been living in my empty nest for several months, talked to experts, and talked to other women in various stages of parenting, and I knew I wasn't going to start feeling better unless I started putting myself—my needs, my priorities—first. Still, I couldn't seem to figure out *how* to do that more quickly than I'd managed so far.

Waiting for My New Life to Begin

The single biggest feeling the empty-nest women I've spoken to expressed, even for those who initially are thrilled to have some time of their own, is a sense of stillness. It sneaks up slowly for some; for others, it's waiting when they return home from dropping their kids off. So how do you get over the shift from being on call to not being called at all? It's an adjustment, and any adjustment takes time. You'll find yourself creating a new rhythm that can take anywhere from a few days to a few months. For some, it may take even longer and require the help of a professional counselor.

Whether you work full-time, part-time, or not at all, whether you volunteer, are a caregiver to an ailing parent, are married or single—before you can transition, you need to give yourself permission to let the spotlight shine on you and become your own role model. Don't worry, you're still there for your children, but as the experts say, this time around in the role of mentor.

Jane Pauley recommends movement. "As a mom a decade out, I've seen varying degrees of struggle among my women friends who've made that transition—and no advice I'd give would have changed the varying degrees of their struggles," she says. "But I will say that when it feels like the struggle is the defining feature of your life, it's probably time to do something. Anything. I saw this idea forming in the mind of a woman who'd heard me speak about my book. She told me, 'I guess the key to moving forward is to *move*.'"

So how do you find the will to turn thoughts into something tangible? This will to move is, no doubt, the hardest part. It's that vulnerability again, but without an understanding of how we can use it to give us the courage and permission we need to try new things, to get up and out. Dr. Barbara Greenberg says it helps to think back to your childhood—ask yourself what you used to do that made you happy. She has found that the happiest people are the ones who "return to their playful spirit."

I wasn't exempt from this stillness. There were days I could talk myself out of most everything. And I make a pretty good argument.

⁓

Sleeping alone can take some getting used to. The middle of the bed really is the way to go.

It's not as if my husband and I have shared a bed every single night of our lives together—we haven't, usually because one or the other of us is traveling. That's when I've enjoyed staying up late reading and watching old movies, usually at the same time. But last week, when the ice came and wouldn't leave, when the kids were both away at college and my husband was stuck out of town, it not only wasn't fun, it was downright sobering.

I was all set for the storm—I knew what to do and how to take care of myself. There were candles and flashlights and extra batteries in case the power went out; I'd bought groceries enough to last me the five days it was predicted to stick around; I'd filled my car up with gas; and I'd made sure pipes under the sinks and in the yard would stay warm. But I couldn't sleep.

Instead, I focused on all the worst-case scenarios. And how big this average-sized house was without anyone inside but me.

Outside, the streets were empty. I couldn't have walked to a neighbor's even if I wanted to—it was far too slippery. Had I fallen, nobody would've found me for a day at least. Everyone I knew locally was stuck at home too, or worse, stuck somewhere other than home. My kids were far away and hadn't a clue. Why would they? Who gets iced in for days in Texas?

We'd had plenty of "snow days" when the kids were little. That's when we lived on the East Coast and celebrated days off from school. It gave us time to forget about the routines that framed our lives. Even when the power went out, we made do together.

Now, it was just me. In the middle of the bed. And I wasn't celebrating. I was just plain bummed.

I thought about how my house and lifestyle were designed for raising kids who no longer live here except for school breaks. And in the cold and with the craziness that comes from being iced in and alone for too many days, I faced what I've been avoiding for months: I'm not just waiting around for the storm to pass or for my husband to come home so I can slide over to my side of the bed—I'm waiting for my new life to begin. To figure out where to go from here—the work I want to do and maybe even the city I want to do it in.

It's my own fault... "Here" came faster than I expected, in spite of the fact that I made a conscious effort to transition to this empty nest. I've done it successfully in most other aspects regarding my kids and my relationship with my husband, but not this one. And it makes me feel as if I have failed.

Silly, really. I help other people do this—move forward, find their voice, their niche... I did it for my own kids. Why can't I do it for me?

Am I hesitant to make the wrong choice at this stage of my life? Probably. Feeling a bit like a dinosaur? Absolutely. Hey, I still prefer to print out everything I read for work and edit it with a pencil and pink eraser. I want to be able to flip real pages. There's no way you'll convince me that doing this on a computer is as satisfying or as effective.

I know what you're thinking...but it's not true. I like change, I do. I've changed the length of my hair, the cut of my jeans, my lipstick color. But this change is different. It's not superficial. It's more than skin deep. It's about me and who I am and what I want to represent. And it's probably my last big career change before I don't have a choice. It's hard to admit, but that's the truth about careers and aging. If I were an actress, I'd likely only get the parts of older women and mothers.

I know what I like to do, what I'm good at, what I'm not good at, what I'm still curious about, and what I will no longer give up. I've read countless quotes about midlife and reinvention and perused the blogs and websites. And I've got something left to accomplish. I do. Still, mine has been an untraditional route to storytelling. I left a full-time career to raise my family, taking on freelance gigs to help support us, to keep me connected to my "voice" and to the world I left behind. But it's not the same as going into an office every day. At least not to the people who hire you.

I also know I'm fortunate in that I've been able to make some choices. But like a lot of moms, I did my share of juggling and then some. The journey was long and complicated and one that I chose at a point in our lives when it was clear that something had to give. And I don't regret it. But I'm not twenty-five anymore. I have two sons in college. A husband. Responsibilities. And truth be told, I suppose, some dreams yet to be realized.

In the past, I put 150 percent of me, of my energy, into whatever I've done. But my energy is different now. It's coupled with decades of experience and learned wisdom. This time around, I'm looking for balance, and hopefully I'll find it before bad weather rolls in again.

I'd better get out of bed.

～

PART THREE

SEARCHING FOR A NEW LIFE WITH MEANING (AND MORE SLEEP)

Building a Bridge

I became a "we" when my husband and I married, though I was careful to maintain my sense of self. But truth be told, the last time I truly felt like an "I" was in 1991, before the positive pregnancy test taken in the bathroom stall at work. Nearly nine months later, "we" were a family. Soon after, my second son came along, and our "we" expanded to four. Now, my family is in retrograde—still a "we," but only of two, except for holidays and semester breaks.

In the end, you raised a family, with or without a job, and now the family is living apart, and your presence is not required day-to-day. So you *do* have time to pursue something new, preferably something that makes you happy. It's the bridge that will take you to the other side—the side of you that is not about being a mom but about being completely you. And remember: no regrets. Learn from the past and move on—don't dwell in it.

When I began to build my own bridge, construction came in fits and starts. As usual, my to-do lists were made in my head when I was falling asleep. They were often interrupted by calls from my kids, who were dealing with a variety of college issues and working hard to handle them, but either needed an ear or just thought it was easier to call than get another text from me to check in. In addition to making mind lists, my bridge included saying yes to new things, attending a conference or two, making travel plans, and moving our living room furniture around (then three months later, moving it all back). I also got pickier and said no to freelance jobs I didn't want to do and to sweeping up dust balls. Now, I pretend to *not* see them just like the rest of my family. And dinner? There's lots of breakfast food. In essence, my bridge from the old me to the new me was paved with pebbles I sorted through. I asked myself questions about old habits and tasks and whether they were relevant anymore. I also thought more about my own childhood, looked at old family movies, at photographs, and revisited my past to better understand why I was a stickler today for so many things, why I was the person I was, and how I could use that foundation (my youth) to transition to my new life. I'd done it when I started this journey as a new mom—the revisionist parenting we talked about earlier. I looked to my upbringing to consider what I did and didn't want to repeat with my own kids.

Now, I needed to do something similar on my own behalf for my next stage of life. Especially where it concerned friendships, something I'd been thinking a lot about. Time is a helpful tool—it offers a chance to stroll down memory lane, then return with valuable information you may not have realized you had all along.

~

It was the sixties and early seventies. We played outside without sunscreen on or our parents around. Our town homes, in the southwest portion of Washington, DC, were modest but new, and our community was fairly well integrated. After school and on weekends, we literally walked out of our front doors and onto the sprawling concrete courtyard where kids of all ages gathered for a game of kickball, catch, or Miss Mary Mack. We rode our bikes around the square, roller-skated, and made up songs. We knew no "bad" words, if you don't count "stupid," which we used with wild abandon. My knees, perpetually scraped from falls, were cleaned by my own spit. At dinnertime, a symphony of parental voices called us to return home, where we did what our parents told us to: wash, eat, complete our thirty minutes of homework, and, if we were good, return outside to play until it was time for bed.

There were sleepovers, frozen-dinner Fridays, entire days spent at the community pool, and a general feeling that we were an extended family. I'm still in touch with some of the people I knew during those years. Our shared experiences sealed our bond. It was a city life created by our politically active parents (though I had no idea they were so at the time), with a dash of suburban influence. Dash, because we knew nothing of malls, good school systems, or garages. All of which I discovered after I graduated from high school.

I know how much our parents influence us, but what about our childhood friendships? How much do they influence the friends we make later in life? For me, growing up in a culturally diverse city with parents who had a very adult-focused home and nontraditional jobs made it difficult as an adult to find other people I could relate to, especially when I lived in different environments—a more rural community, and then again later in a suburban one, where conformity is key to fitting in.

Today, my closest friends are my aunts and uncles and a couple of writers. They too had upbringings that were nontraditional in many ways, and we speak the same language without trying. It's not that I'm opposed to trying harder and expanding my circle—I have and do. It's just I've grown weary of the initial phase of a new friendship when you're trying to assess whether there is enough in common, whether it's worth the effort or if they've already formed and sealed their inner circle. No one ever actually says that out loud, but it's true—it's what everyone does, especially after a major stage of life, such as parenting, has ended. Some people are open to new relationships, and some less so.

The Father Factor

It occurred to me one evening, after too many cups of caffeinated hot tea, that there were aspects of my childhood and my relationship with my father that were still affecting me all these years later—and hindering the next stage of life. I needed to work through them and move on. I read various books and articles on father/daughter relationships, analyzed my own, and talked and wrote about my feelings until I began to gain a clearer understanding of how unhelpful it is to let cruddy feelings keep resurfacing. But when women with similar father/daughter issues end up sharing their stories with me, it always brings me back home.

After teaching essay writing to adults for many years, I've found that the majority of my students are over forty, female, and have had less than ideal father/daughter relationships. These women are in search of their voice and don't want to spend another decade keeping it bottled up. Sometimes the classes are liberating for them—a way to better understand who they are, where they've been, and how to transition to whatever is next. It was in one of these writing workshops that one of my students—a woman I assumed to be in her forties—mentioned she was back in college, making up for lost time and trying to figure out what to do with the rest of her life. She was in my class because she said she had lots of funny stories to tell and she wasn't sure where to start. The more she spoke, the more I sensed something that wasn't humor at all but a mask for what was hidden—something painful that was only now beginning to surface.

When we were in the middle of a group exercise designed to draw the students out, I took a leap of faith and asked if she had a father who was fully present growing up, if she'd had what I called "father love."

You could have heard a pin drop.

"No," she said flatly.

Then she went on to explain that her father, who was emotionally unstable and unwell, had left when she was very young. He resurfaced when she was a teenager, and she tried to help him by being his caretaker for many years.

Suddenly, the room full of fifteen women and one man—most of whom were middle-aged, many of whom were empty nesters who had never met one another previously—began to open up. And as they spoke, the subject of fathers stirred the most emotion. Some talked about how their fathers were alcoholics, others that they were absent or angry, and yes, some were loving. All of their fathers impacted their lives in ways they wanted to explore in their writing.

The idea that the father/daughter relationship is as important, if not more so, than the mother/daughter relationship was not spoken about much among my parents' generation. This may be because of the more traditional role mothers played in the past, raising children. Most women of that era didn't tell their husbands what they expected of them as a parent.

Years ago, I heard a pediatrician interviewed on a radio show talk about father/daughter relationships. She said that a girl's experience of parental love with her dad pretty much serves as the model of what male love is all about, and if it's a positive experience, she'll do better later in life—that his love can help make or break her self-esteem. I can relate.

~

The pool table he gave me for my first house sat smack-dab in the middle of the basement floor, an otherwise furniture-less space, devoid of purpose, really, except as a pass-through to the utility room. I put the "table" there, all six by twelve inches of it, because I am his daughter and because, though he was prone to making me cry, he knew how to make me laugh. And I did, each time I came down to do the laundry.

It wasn't the only gift I received from my father. He had been using gift-giving as an excuse to feed his addiction to mail order since I was little. But when my brother, sister, and I moved away to begin our own lives as adults, he delighted in finding objects that ended up as conversation starters when company came.

There was the alarm clock that crowed like a rooster and that I could not turn off; the electric socks that burned my feet; the shirts with monogrammed cuffs for my husband; the monkey glasses from the Museum of Modern Art; and the dozens of knockoff Rolex and designer watches. After he got sick, he gave envelopes filled with objects he picked up along the way, all, ironically, more valuable to me than the purchased gifts—"S" clips, as he called them (paper clips to those not as poetic about such things), rubber bands, and hand wipes from the gas stations he frequented.

His need to buy was genetic. His parents owned a small department store in Brooklyn. For years, they lived in an apartment above the store, and he spent most of his free time working there. His mother's philosophy was that life is about finding a bargain and then buying two. Each purchase seemed to make her happier than the previous one, and though she rarely used any of the many things she acquired, she seldom, if ever, parted with them either. I always assumed she was stockpiling her own happiness. When she became too ill to care for herself, my aunt and uncle boxed it all up and gave it to charity, ultimately making many people happy, or happier, as the case may be.

My father's shopping was a process—he loved ordering and then passing the item along, especially if it amused him. Most of his gifts were purchased with little thought for the interests or needs of the recipient. Each time he gave me something, I recalled the game I played when I was a girl with my friend Thomasine. "He loves me, he loves me not," we'd chant, pulling petals from a flower one at a time, until the last petal revealed the truth. If we had no real flowers, we'd make our own out of construction paper, usually rigging them to end just the way we wanted. Mostly, we were petal-pulling about one of the Beatles, or Davy Jones of the Monkees. Sometimes, when I was alone, I'd pull petals about my father, especially after he called me stupid or a moron. Then he'd bang on my bedroom door and apologize and call me "Missy Sweetie" and take me to buy a doll.

When I was in my late twenties, my father had open-heart surgery. In the ICU, with our family taking turns visiting, my mother held his left hand in hers, caressing his wedding ring, which he had refused to remove. He responded to her touch, to her words, till they had soothed him enough to fall back to sleep. When it was my turn to say hello, I stood next to him, unsure of what to say or do. We rarely hugged or touched unless we were sad. I had always longed for a father-knows-best to guide me in my life, to tell me why I was special and worthwhile, but his talent lay mostly in empathizing when I was hurt, because (as I came to learn) he had endured so much emotional pain of his own growing up.

When I was twenty-five, I ditched my dreams of working in advertising in New York after my engagement to a man there fell apart. My father borrowed a van and drove from Washington to collect me. He emptied my apartment of all that I had, which took less than an hour, the last item being my wedding shoes, still in the box. I looked on, startled, as he carried them as if they were Cinderella's slippers, tears streaming down his ruddy cheeks. Back at my parents' house, I collapsed for weeks and spoke to nobody, my father fielding every call. When I cried in my sleep, he'd open the door to check on me, though he never came in, and I never admitted I saw him standing there.

Now, in the ICU, it was my turn. I stroked his hand, once, twice. Then I sat next to him and began to chat nervously about my new job and things I thought might amuse him. His heart had been taken out and put back in, tubes everywhere, an aneurysm repaired, triple bypass performed. He looked pale and weak and incapable of mail-ordering anything ever again. Of being angry ever again. And then, suddenly, he opened his eyes, turned to me, and said, "Stop it! Don't hold my hand!" And he shook free of mine.

Not long after he recovered, my father was presented with an award during a special ceremony. Family and friends came. He asked me to invite as many people as I could to fill the place up so he would look good. And so I did. As he gave his speech, he said thanks to people I did not know, and to my mother, and my sister, and my brother. When it was all done, I went home. The phone rang. It was my friend Roseanne, who had been at the event at my request. "He mentioned everyone but you," she said.

"I know," I replied. "I know."

When my second child was born by C-section, I lay awake in the hospital for several nights, unable to find a painkiller that quelled the knifelike feeling in my gut. Though the nurses had opened the windows and set up fans, the broken air conditioning on my floor made the darkness seem to last forever. I called my father, a man who loved the telephone and rarely slept himself. "Hi, Dad, it's me—I can't sleep," I said. "And neither can the rest of the city, from what I see out of my window." His interest piqued, he asked me to tell him about it. And so, at one o'clock in the morning, I did. About the man in a business suit in the office building I saw across the street. About the other men in suits who came and went into his office, about all the telephones and computers I could see lit up. He imagined aloud that they were drug dealers, all up to no good, or bookies, or the CIA, and his stories lulled me to sleep.

Years later, when my sons and I went to California to visit my parents, my father grew irritated with my mother, ironically about her inability to place a Happy Meal order at a McDonald's drive-through. He called her names. I begged him to stop, especially in front of my children. His angry reply hit me like a bullet, shattering all the progress I hoped we had made over the years. He turned his wrath on me, called me stupid and a moron, said I was the same dumb kid as always. Then he announced he was not going to talk to me ever again.

A few months later, I received a package addressed to my sons. Inside were train sets that he asked me to give them when they were older. I stared at the phone until I gathered the nerve and called him. "Hi, Dad," I said, my voice breaking, and thanked him for the gifts. Why not come to visit us, I suggested, and give the boys the trains himself?

"I'd like to," he said, "but I'm not sure how much longer I'll be around. I just wanted to make sure they had something to open after I'm gone. You have terrific boys." Two months later, he died.

To this day, no matter how I rig the petals of a flower, I still don't know if he loved me or loved me not.

Throughout my life, when my mother wasn't up for answering a personal question, she'd say, "It's complicated." I'm not a big fan of the expression (though the movie was pretty good), but when someone asks me about my own relationship with my father, I have to resist the urge to answer with, "It's complicated." Now, and for the sisterhood, seems as good a time as any to explain why.

Sometimes, after we grow up, we figure out that the people who were charged with taking care of us were not necessarily ready for the role. They focused mostly on themselves for a variety of reasons, some having to do with a lack of childhood of their own and their subsequent need to be center stage as an adult. Toss in issues of temperament, especially at a time when talking about behavior and feelings were not the norm, and you have my father. There were days when he was the greatest, funniest human on the planet, and others when he was the polar opposite. Through trial and error, I learned to never completely let my guard down, because I wasn't quite sure which father he was going to be when I rose in the morning or came home in the afternoon. I only knew that whatever he was angry about was my fault, because that's what he told me, and nobody else told me otherwise. It wasn't until I found love, a career, and good friends that I finally understood that his behavior had nothing to do with me.

My father's impact on me was profound but in ways I've only recently come to terms with. So I made a promise to myself to love my children differently—to be fully present, consider who they are as individuals, and value them, every single day.

When my father passed away, my children were still very young. It was, perhaps, my last major life transition until my sons left for college. Before then, I hadn't thought much about life as a series of transitions. Milestones, yes. Transitions, not so much.

Today, for me, the word "transition" implies navigating through something that's difficult. Something, perhaps, that you'd rather not have to experience (in a perfect world) but that is a natural part of life. My father's passing was one such transition.

The thing about a transition is that it provides opportunities to revisit the past and leave behind what isn't relevant to your future or what may be preventing you from imagining it. I had done versions of this before—shed a layer, if you will. But after my father died, his physical absence made it easier for me to work through feelings without being swayed by his behavior—he could be very compelling, especially when he was his best, most generous self.

Recently, I thought about my father's passing and a beautiful pen that was dear to him. It reminded me that some endings are actually beginnings in disguise.

~

It's just after midnight at our hotel in San Francisco. Tomorrow is my father's funeral. I've slipped away from the bed where my husband sleeps, our two young sons (ages two and four) inches away, and into the tiny bathroom to write. Earlier today, surprising even myself, I told my family I wanted to speak at his service. They had correctly assumed that the previous me—the one who found it difficult to use my voice in his presence—wouldn't, couldn't. But they don't know me now—the woman with a career, a family, and an identity far and apart from her father's.

The floor of the hotel bathroom is cold and clammy beneath me. With my father's Montblanc, I begin to write his eulogy. The pen was among the piles on his crowded dresser top in my parent's apartment in California. There were newspaper clippings; quotes scribbled on yellow, lined paper; locks of hair belonging to my sister and my youngest son; my father's military dog tags; and an array of cheap watches. Foraging through it all, my mother pulled out a burgundy pen—most likely a knockoff, knowing his penchant for finding deep discounts—and handed it to me. "I'd like you to have it," she said, then added quickly, "Your father would have wanted you to have it."

As I write, I become aware of the power at my fingertips, the power of the written word using a tool he once used. Ours was a difficult relationship. Do I focus on the good?

I write about the weekend road trips to state fairs and to the mountains, about our family of five redheads' sunburnt adventure to Curacao, about the endless movie nights and bottomless bowls of popcorn, and about cupboards brimming with his favorites: canned tuna, artichoke hearts, and chocolate-covered marshmallows with graham cracker crusts.

My friends said they envied me. How I was allowed to stay up late and watch Johnny Carson and Dick Cavett. How we had a house full of telephones and a Ping-Pong table from Sears that we sometimes put on our tiny patch of lawn while surprised strangers drove by and watched us play.

I write about how my father rose early to drive me to school when it rained. And how he sometimes played cards with me and shared cookies, which he placed on the Style section of the *Washington Post*, reading in between turns. These memories all come flooding out, my tears as well, mopped up by the roll of toilet paper at hand.

In the morning, as my mother, sister, brother, and I approach the funeral home, I see a hearse, and men clad in black unloading a coffin. I wasn't there when he stopped breathing and slumped over his newspaper at the dining room table; when my mother tried to revive his heart that had been bypassed years before; when my sister, driving at breakneck speed to get to his side, pulled into the parking lot of their community to see him being loaded into an ambulance; when they both learned he was not coming back. I was, instead, thousands of miles away, blowing bubbles with my boys in the hot summer sun after spending the week taking care of my maternal grandmother, my Nana, hospitalized for the first time in her life.

When the call came, I thought it must be her and raced to answer. And now here I am, staring at a coffin, a coffin that must be my father's.

"That's Dad. Oh my God, that's Dad," I cry out, and though it's my father whose heart has stopped, it's me who cannot breathe.

At the funeral home, when it's time to take my place on the podium in front of the small gathering, I stand, wobbly at first, then resolute. And I recite the good during what becomes a practice session of sorts for the memorial service that will be held six weeks from now, thousands of miles away in Washington, DC, where my parents built their lives before moving out west.

After the funeral, at the burial site, my father's five grandsons hop, skip, and jump over tiny tombstones that mark the graves of children. The seriousness of the day has gone over their heads, and they revel in the camaraderie of their cousins.

As the coffin is lowered into the ground, each child tosses a long-stemmed sunflower on top, and each adult a shovelful of dirt, until Dad reaches his final resting place, and I turn away.

Back at home on the East Coast, the time between the funeral in San Francisco and the memorial in Washington, DC, seems endless, and the quiet of our rural home provides no comfort.

In my younger days, I would have welcomed the silence. Throughout my childhood, I fell asleep to the glass-clinking, name-dropping, joke-cracking sounds of my parents' Washington parties. There was a lot of talk filled with words I didn't understand. How I wished all those voices would leave my house in peace and take their smelly cigars and Chanel No. 5 with them. There was one voice louder than the others—it belonged to my father. Now he's gone, and who would have guessed—it's too quiet to sleep.

At the memorial, in front of a much larger crowd, I read the eulogy. My voice is strong and clear.

While house-hunting several months later, my husband and I find a tiny, dilapidated place in the country with a barn and stables. I remove the Montblanc from my purse and step out of the car, holding it tightly. As we walk up a hill, I think about how much my father would have enjoyed the view.

Suddenly, everywhere I turn, I see his face—his long and ruddy nose and his large handlebar mustache. A mustache that I trimmed at his request, but also so I could be close to him. Then, when we return to the car, I open my hand. The pen is gone. How could something so physically obvious vanish into thin air?

Sometimes a loss leads to something new. Though I can't hear my father's voice anymore, I've finally found my own.

~

As a writer, teacher, daughter, and new empty-nester in search of my future, I've learned a lot about self-esteem and the power of love. If I could pass along a message to all my sisters out there who've felt the pain and shame of a poor father/daughter relationship, the message would be in two parts:

1. It's not your fault. You were just a kid. All kids deserve to be loved and protected. Don't blame yourself for what your father did or didn't do, what he said or didn't say.

2. Write about it, talk about it, or turn it into art. By sharing our wounds, we open up our hearts, and healing happens. I know—I've seen it firsthand.

The bottom line is this: a negative relationship with your father doesn't need to define you. As mature adults, we have the power to set the course of our lives. Remember that—we have the power.

Doing Things Differently

I'd grown bored of yogurt and raisin toast and no longer had the crusts of my kid's sandwiches to finish, so I could either starve or say yes to what I considered a cliché—doing lunch.

~

My kids are leaving the nest, so I go out to lunch now and again with grown-ups to try and remember what life was like before chicken nuggets. Last week, I ate lunch with two friends who are writers, both of whom happen to be men. We went to La Madeleine, a popular French bistro chain, where the servers wear those big poufy hats. Here's what I discovered:

1. Leopard print is the new black. It must be. I saw it on women's sandals, purses, blouses, and pants. It was paired with other prints, with solids, with more leopard prints. It looked sexy. It looked bold. It looked to be in fashion, or maybe I just time-traveled to Florida (no offense, Florida). Regardless, I felt under-dressed and definitely did not get the memo. At what age do you start to get the memo?

2. You can have a nice tush when you're over fifty. There were some

very nice tushes in line waiting to get their lunch. I know because I was sitting on a bench waiting for one of my friends, and I was like, right there, at eye level—so trust me, I couldn't avoid noticing. I tried, because I really wanted to see what desserts were in the dessert case, but my view was obscured by all those tushes. They defied the stereotype of older women sagging in all the wrong places. They're rockin' fifty-plus. It's inspiring.

3. I've always known that women have a lot of things in their purse "just in case," because I too subscribe to the notion that you can never be too prepared, but I never knew that an electronic card shuffler was one of those things. Now I do. And that women whip them out to play cards after lunch at certain places where salads are served.

4. Men are eating lunch somewhere else. Presumably somewhere that serves more meat, usually with barbecue sauce. Maybe that's just Texas, but I don't think so. All told, I saw maybe two men in this place, in addition to the two men I was with, which, by the way, made four men in a restaurant with maybe one hundred women, mostly eating salads. Either the men there were very smart, or they had no choice. After all, we women can be *very* persuasive. Especially if we're wearing leopard prints. Grrr.

5. If you're a woman and you try to pull two small tables together that may potentially block an emergency exit, all the women at nearby tables will tell you that you cannot block an emergency exit. Then they will stare you down until you find another spot. Grrr.

6. Soup does not fill you up. But since everyone else is eating salads, you may feel guilty for wanting to eat pastries afterward. So instead, you will go home and eat two ice-cream sandwiches. And follow it with a large glass of milk. But you

will still remember the soup fondly. And you'll decide that next time you visit, you'll wear something leopardy and tap into your inner animal, which will make you feel bolder about ordering a pastry, even though someone may be sitting on a bench and surveying your tush.

7. I'm sure cavewomen paid attention to their feet, buffing their calloused heels with a T. rex molar, but today's women have stepped up their game. I saw nails of every color—with sparkles, with patterns—and not a corn to be seen. Even (of course) leopard print. These are not my grandmother's toes. Go ahead, do a Google image search for "pretty toenail designs." You won't believe it.

～

Okay, maybe I wasn't quite ready to step up my leopard-print game, but my transition did include trying new things. The goal was to get out of my comfort zone. I was never a fan of going to the gym, but I had grown up taking ballet. I'd also tried Pilates and dabbled in yoga a few times, though not in any meaningful way. I was too impatient. But this time, this time was different. I willed myself to try harder. Who knew?

～

I'm not proud of it: sometimes I make grunting noises when I bend over to pick something up. The same kinds of noises made by people twenty-five years my senior. For someone who once danced regularly, who was fluid and quiet as a mouse while dancing, let's just say I'm somewhat surprised. Age, it seems, really does catch up to us. If I were a door, I'd spray myself with WD-40.

Last month, I decided to do something about my inability to bend quietly and thought that yoga might be the cure. My doctor has been encouraging me to try it again, but I've been hesitant to be part of a class setting. What if I can't do something? How embarrassing would that be? And what if I make those awful noises while doing it?

Several years ago, I'd tried two informal yoga sessions led by a friend and then moved on to teaching myself the basics while watching a yoga DVD (which my husband also watched while sitting on the couch, eating popcorn and correcting my form). But that experiment lasted about two days.

It was clear that I needed to try harder and take a class with actual people, in an actual classroom. I told myself that if I can't strike a pose, I can just modify it; we're not all Gumby, right?

So I looked through the brochure from my local recreation center for a beginner's course and discovered that yoga is no longer just yoga. Yoga is Ashtanga Yoga, Fluid Motion Yoga, Power Yoga, Prenatal Yoga, Hatha Yoga, Iyengar Yoga, Vinyasa Flow Yoga, Yoga for Fitness, Yoga Stretch, Yoga Mixed, and YogaBody Express.

I settled on Hatha Yoga, which was noted as being "smart and safe yoga." Call me Goldilocks, but that sounded just right. I convinced a friend of mine, who also makes noises when she bends over, to take it as well. Then she convinced her friend to join us. A yoga posse we were.

Off we went with our mats, blankets, stretchy pants, and a fair amount of anxiety. Between us, we had bad shoulders, knees, backs, and necks—as it turns out, just like everyone else in the class.

The students range in age from maybe thirty to seventy. Some people have taken the same beginners class for years. Others are new, like us. Of the sixteen people in the class, three are guys. I've learned a lot about some of the people, not because I've actually spoken with them, but because yoga, it seems, inspires a whole host of noises, not all of them being a groan while bending over.

During the last few minutes of each class, the teacher turns the lights down and the new-age music up. We lie on our mats and follow her instructions to be still and mindful. One woman in the class falls asleep within a minute of starting this. I know she falls asleep because when she does, she snores. Not a gentle snore, mind you, but more of a deviated septum sort of snore. At one point, I wondered if I should wake her up—could wake her up. Then the music ended, and a teeny tiny barely audible chime sounded, and just like that the snoring stopped, and she was alert.

Yoga is all about the breathing, and I've found that some people take the "deep" part of the instructor's deep-breathing reminders quite literally. They very loudly and purposefully suck in all the air around them for a few counts and then release it for a few counts, all around them—onto their yoga-class neighbors.

Last but not least, there are the students who clearly registered for Hatha Yoga by mistake, thinking perhaps they were actually signing up for Breakwinda Yoga, which wasn't on the list but probably should be. Because, well, you can probably guess. They get *very* relaxed. Especially when their knees are bent or they are doing downward dog.

Recently, I was sandwiched between the woman with the septum issue and one of the Breakwinda Yoga students. The twelve-year-old in me covered my nose with my blanket and got a wicked case of the giggles. I dared not let my eyes meet my friend's. Or her friend's. Let's just say that had my sons been with me, things could have deteriorated rapidly.

So if you've been afraid of taking a yoga class because you're worried you can't do something right or might make noises trying it, I'm here to tell you, that's not a good enough excuse. I do recommend you bring something to cover your face, however, just in case you too find yourself in a class with students who have registered for the wrong type of yoga.

~

The Power of Positive Thinking

For years, we've told our children to pay attention, to tune in. Now, we need to remind ourselves to do the same.

One of the basic tenets of psychology is that what you focus on grows in significance. So if you're focusing on something negative, it can cloud all your thoughts. To bring about change, especially during times of change, such as when your children are leaving home, begin by shifting your focus away from how difficult you think it will be to adapt to their leaving to more positive and productive thoughts. What do you want to change about your life? What are you curious about? The experts say if you can shut out the negative noise, envision what you want, and pursue an interest, you're well on your way—intentionally moving toward something instead of intentionally staying still.

I've been guilty of wallowing in the very thing that is bringing me down: buying into it, overanalyzing, staying so absorbed in whatever it is (the wrong kind of focusing) that days and weeks pass, and I've wasted a ridiculous amount of time and accomplished nothing. That said, I'm not always receptive to people who make copious suggestions about thinking on the brighter side and who start singing that song from *Frozen*: "Let it go, let it go…" You know what I mean. You respond to every one of their well-meaning suggestions with, "Yes, but…" thinking they have no idea what you're going through and how nothing they're saying applies to you or your situation. This is because you're in the groove of being

bummed and cannot accept that there is anything you can possi-
bly do to affect change. Especially if there are other forces at work
that you don't have a say in or control over. The truth is, in most
cases, there *is* something you can do. Here are some approaches to
giving yourself a boost—they've worked for me and others—from
the more traditional to the slightly less so:

- **Exercise.** Any kind of exercise. The point is to tune in to your
  movement, the music you listen to while exercising, whatever
  rings your bell so you *stop* thinking about the junk that doesn't.
  Besides yoga, I walk. I've even been known to walk up and
  down the steps in my house repeatedly when I don't have time
  to go outside for a longer trek.

- **Do something artful.** Take photographs. Get lost in it. Draw,
  paint, hammer, bake, cook. Focus on the joy of it, and tune
  everything else out.

- **Practice gratitude.** I don't mean to sound like a greeting card
  here, but when you think things are awful, say exactly how they're
  awful, out loud, without anyone around. Use all the bad words
  you want. No one is listening. Then do the opposite: say out
  loud what's *good* about your life. What things you appreciate—
  and by appreciate, I mean the people, the love, the objects (yes,
  the shoes), good health, humor, knowledge, pets, family, music,
  beauty. Sometimes you have to dump what's making you blue to
  see what's true. Okay, maybe that's a greeting card.

- **Eat something you loved to eat as a child.** Rice pudding, for
  example. It works for me. Not massive quantities, of course,
  because then you'll have other issues. Just eat enough to make
  you remember a time in your life, or people in your life, who
  brought you joy. Reconnect.

- **Go to a museum.** Lose yourself in the object, the history, the stories.
- **Hang out with the funniest person you know.** Seriously. If you can't, rent a movie that makes you laugh and fast-forward to your favorite lines. Or open a favorite book and read the lines that make you laugh out loud. There are scenes in the movie *Mother* that still make me laugh, and I've watched it more times than I should probably admit.
- **Take a shower.** It's soothing and quieting and the best place I know to shut out the noise without leaving home.
- **If you still can't shift your focus, then counter it.** Ask yourself what you're most worried about, then how likely the scenarios are to come true. Then take it even further: if they did come true, how would you approach solutions? Imagine the worst-case scenario, and solve it. By doing this, you remember that whatever life zings you with, you can zing it back, regain a sense of control, and get your confidence back besides.

If you've tried these methods but are still finding it difficult to maintain your motivation and a positive view of the future, there's more you can do. It involves some self-analysis of sorts.

In his book, *The Emotional Life of Your Brain: How Its Unique Patterns Affect the Way You Think, Feel, and Live—and How You Can Change Them*, Dr. Richard Davidson, professor of psychology and psychiatry at the University of Wisconsin-Madison, says that through his research, he's found that we all have a particular and "consistent way of responding to the experiences of our lives." He calls these responses our emotional style. There are six styles in all, and we're each a unique mix of some more than others: resilience, outlook, social intuition, self-awareness, sensitivity to context, and attention. For some, emotional style can make life (and sometimes other people's lives) quite challenging, so by understanding what our particular style/mix is, we can use that knowledge, if we so desire, to accept who we are or to change it. In essence, we can help ourselves by recognizing our emotional patterns of reacting to situations and then adjust them, with the goal of being happier and more productive.

Two of these six styles are particularly important to helping us during the transition away from full-time parenting toward our new, more singularly focused lives. They are resilience (how you recover from adversity) and outlook (how long you maintain positive emotion). Do you wallow in something that happens or quickly move on? I'm a wallower. There are negatives and positives to both extremes. Are you a glass-half-full or glass-half-empty kind of person? Again, there are negatives and positives to both. The bottom line is that these styles can affect how well you make and accept change.

Davidson provides a variety of strategies to help modify your outlook and resilience styles. For the purpose of aiding you through the transition process, I've adapted them with the goal in mind of increasing your resilience and outlook (becoming happier). They go beyond general advice to specific exercises you can try at home.

How to Become More Resilient

The first and most important thing to know about becoming an empty nester is that nobody expects you to transition immediately. It's a thoroughly human experience, and as Davidson says, "You need to be able to feel and respond to your own emotions, which is difficult to do if you move on too quickly." That said, if you're having difficulty moving forward, you may also have trouble achieving what you'd like to do next in life. Again, there is a scientific explanation for this and evidence to boot—a brain "signature," if you will. So what can you do to become more resilient and help yourself move forward after the kids leave (or in preparation for them leaving)? Davidson recommends something called *mindfulness meditation*. It's a very simple process, he says, but it does require practice, and one size does not fit all. "Each person must find what's best for her," he points out. Mindfulness can be helpful because it allows people to focus on present-moment awareness instead of focusing on the past and worrying about the future. You can find free guided meditations at www.marc.ucla .edu. You can also try these three basic steps, which I've adapted and used many times:

1. Sit someplace where you are comfortable, but your posture is good (erect). A chair, the floor, your bed. Close your eyes.
2. Breathe normally. Place your hands on your abdomen so you can feel how it moves with each breath.
3. If you have thoughts that distract you, become aware of your breathing again and refocus on that instead.

Start small (two minutes) because, as Davidson says, "No one can say you don't have two minutes. Then expand and do it for longer and longer periods of time." I thought meditation was all a bunch of hocus-pocus for a long time. When I took that yoga class, it incorporated some meditation. Every time the teacher said to do things like become aware of my tongue or my belly, I'd start laughing. Then I went to a class where none of my friends were present, and man, I had been crazy stressed, and my body hurt from

the stress. This time, I tuned into her words. I followed the instructions to a T, so that when my mind began to wander, I refocused
on the breathing. What a concept—what a crazy, simple concept.
And don't you know, I felt my tongue relax. I didn't even know
it was up at the roof of my mouth until it wasn't. My shoulders
relaxed. They had been up by my ears. And by the end of class, I
felt more in control of my body. As if I could, at will, make myself
chill, whether my body wanted to or not. And after I chilled, I was
happier. Turns out there's power in the release. Funny how that
works. You feel stronger when you let yourself relax. Because you're
tuned in, not tuned out.

What if you're plagued with thoughts that you're not good enough
or smart enough to move forward and realize your dreams? "When
we lack confidence, we lack positive thoughts," says Davidson. "Just
regard them as thoughts—not better or worse thoughts. When you
do this, you begin to rapidly transform—they lose their power to
hijack you." By letting it be, we are not agreeing with the thought,
just sort of neutralizing it. It gives us time to pause, and when we do,
we become aware of the unpleasantness and have a chance to move
beyond it to a happier place.

How to Improve Your Outlook

How we approach our future and the level of happiness we feel
and maintain can be daunting after the kids leave, especially if
our natural tendency is to be less optimistic rather than more.
Suppose you're initially excited to have more time on your
hands, to start a new job, find a job, etc., but within days, you've
lost that enthusiasm and are just plain bummed and sitting still.
To keep yourself motivated may take more than a brownie and a

new purse. It may take a little science. And actually, that purse (eventually)...

Davidson's research has shown that by raising activity in the regions of our brain associated with planning and our sense of reward, we can experience, for longer periods of time, the happiness we once only felt fleetingly.

In his book, Davidson employs the process of shopping to show how you might benefit from delayed gratification to boost your outlook on life. Simply put, when you buy something you like or want, you generally feel happy. That happiness lasts a little or a long time, depending on your outlook. What if you could extend that good feeling so that it lasts longer? So that every day feels as if you just bought something new, even if you didn't? Applying his technique, here's my take on what you need to do: shop for something you want—at a store or online—but instead of actually purchasing the object of your desire or that brownie (and eating it), just "window shop" without your credit card close at hand. Focus on what you could do with the money you saved or how much healthier you'd feel if you *didn't* give in to the urge to buy it right then and there. This focus—where you purposely imagine your end goal (saving money, fitting into a dress)—helps you to train your brain to perceive gratification differently. The new goal becomes the more desired goal. Now, try the same thing *with* the credit card within reach. It gets harder, perhaps, but ultimately more rewarding the longer you hold out. Do this daily, but eventually, reward yourself in some way. As he says in his book, you have to know that "your imagined future will eventually arrive."

You could also use the same technique for completing tasks

that seem daunting at first, such as applying for a new job, taking classes in something you've always wanted to do, saying hello to new people, etc. Focus on how doing these things is going to enhance your life—where these actions could lead. Again, delaying the gratification and then feeling the joy of experiencing the future you imagined alters your outlook and your sense of self.

Davidson also suggests a technique called well-being therapy developed by Giovanni Fava of the University of Bologna in Italy. Again, like a good recipe and for the purposes of this book, I've modified it a bit:

1. Write down something about yourself that you feel is positive—a characteristic that you think is a strong point. Do this daily. Keep these positive characteristics in a journal, and read them when you are feeling low. I've done this to remind myself of what I'm good at. Sometimes I use humor to amuse myself. As someone with impossibly curly hair, I once wrote, "My hair will never go limp." As someone who can identify even the oddest of odors, I once wrote, "I could have been a nose (a perfumer)." Make it suit your personality.

2. Say "thank you" on a regular basis. When you do, take the time to make eye contact with the person you are thanking, and pay attention to the connection between the two of you. Little moments like this add up and can make a big difference to your day. Sometimes I forget to do this when I'm caught up in my own world.

3. Compliment people and notice their reactions—and yours in return.

"Common-sense changes in one's environment may be helpful as well," says Davidson. These include things like making sure your home or work environment have positive visual reminders of family, friends, places you've been. Change them frequently though, so you don't get so familiar with the images that you don't truly see them anymore. When I stop noticing family photos—take them for granted—I shift them around. "Potentially, these practices help us see this transition with a freshness. They are not going to cure all ills, but they equip people with skills they can turn to," says Davidson.

If, after you've tried some of these techniques, your sadness or depression is interfering with your daily life to the point that you are not functioning and extends to a month or more, it's best to seek the aid of a professional counselor who can help you using behavioral therapy and other techniques.

I know that for many people, finding a counselor, making an appointment, then actually going to the appointment can be the hardest part. But it's always worth the effort, because *you* are worth the effort. Some of the hesitancy may involve the unknown, the *What do they do in those sessions anyway?* kind of questions. With that in mind, I asked Dr. Margaret Rutherford for some examples of how she approaches patients who are in search of their future and their happiness, especially at this stage of life:

If a patient answers the question "What would make you happy now?" with an answer like "If I lost fifty pounds" or "If I had a better marriage" or in this case "If my son/daughter were not gone"...my response would be something like this: "If you are basing your happiness on something you cannot achieve today, then happiness will not be possible."

I ask them to look around and see what they can control in their life. Today. Now. And if there are things connected to that overarching goal of weight loss, a happier marriage, less loneliness—what are those things? What can they do today about it? Make that small behavior change. Or attitude change.

Have one Hershey's kiss instead of the whole bag. Go for a walk, however short. Stop yourself before automatic criticism of your spouse comes out of your mouth. Start giving him affirmation for what he does well. Write a letter to your kid, learn a new skill, make a friend. Grow your own life. Soak up the feelings associated with those small steps. And you are highly likely to feel happier. It may happen slowly, but the process will unfold.

Defining Happiness

"I thought there would be more."

You might remember the line from the movie *Boyhood*—the mom (played by actress Patricia Arquette) says it to her son as he's leaving for college. She's wondering if the best of life is behind her, because ahead of her, all she can see is her own mortality.

The truth is, there *is* more.

Lately, people have asked me about happiness as if I know the secret to finding it. I'm not sure why exactly. There's no smile painted on my face or sign that reads "I'm really happy" around my neck. Perhaps it's a matter of perception—my kids are off to college, and I've been married a long time. I only know that I've done my school-of-hard-knocks research, have generous and loving aunts and uncles who've imparted their wisdom—and that happiness is very different from what I once thought it would be.

~

Before I had kids, I didn't spend much time contemplating my own happiness. I don't mean I didn't want to be happy or wonder if I'd have a happy life—I did. I just expected I'd be happy, because the alternative sucked.

I went about my life and made my share of mistakes, hoping the good stuff would prevail. Sooner or later, it did, and before I knew it, I was in my late twenties, had a career and nice clothes to wear, a decent car, and money to pay for gas. It was all new and exciting, and it felt like happiness—looked like happiness anyway. With the career and clothes and car came more confidence, and with confidence, I met a man and fell in love, and when you're in love, everything seems possible...and that makes you pretty darn happy.

Eventually, I got married, bought a house, had children. Life was full and sweet and good—it was everything I thought it should be. Then, as the years passed, the not-so-good began to happen: there was loss, conflict, sickness. The notion of happiness—was I or wasn't I?—was something I began to question. I thought about all the years I took my happiness for granted. I tried to remember what it was that made me so happy before I started to feel so unhappy. I'd study pictures from my past and think, "That's from when I was happy."

Although people rarely talked about happiness and their true feelings when I was younger, by the time I was in my forties, happiness—or the lack thereof—was all anyone seemed to be talking about. Their story generally began with "If only." If only they had better childhoods, more money, nicer clothes, a better car, a better job (any job), or were prettier. I had my own list of if-onlys, many of which stemmed from my youth and the choices I made, along with storybook assumptions about happiness that didn't include reality, which can bite even the most resilient of us.

Here's what I wish I'd known when I was in the thick of my misery: happiness is a process. It's about constantly adjusting expectations to match your changing truth. At a certain point, if you really want to be happy, you have to choose to be happy. How do you do that? Stop obsessing about what you don't have and focus instead on the good things in your life.

Happiness is not going to hit you over the head—there's no lightning-bolt "happiness" moment. The bad stuff—that's what's going to hit you over the head. You can count on it. But if you spend more time thinking about the dark days than the light, it may keep you from seeing what's right there in front of you.

Your happiness.

～

Mom and former HR manager turned blogger Danyelle Smith Little (http://www.thecubiclechick.com/) knows a thing or two about happiness and the pursuit thereof. As a single teen parent, she realized that her future was dependent not so much on what had happened in the past but on the choices she made going forward— her ability to regroup and bounce back. Eventually, she found a career in HR, got married, and had another child—this time, on her terms. When her company downsized a few years ago and she was laid off, she poured her heart and soul into her blog and helping working moms. When it was time for her son to begin college and pursue his passion for acting, she was supportive: "When I was his age, I couldn't just leave and go try a career—I was a mom. But I wanted him to have that experience. I'm really proud of him for being steadfast." And though it took a while to get used to him being gone, she's learning to let him make his own decisions (and mistakes). The goal is to instill in him the same sense of resiliency and search for happiness that she says has been enormously helpful throughout her life.

Clearly, happiness doesn't just happen. You have to want it—and you have to want to work for it. By midlife, most women have spent time considering what their idea of happiness really is, especially after the children leave home. Popular bloggers have offered opinions and advice on the subject. "Mine are married and gone," says Yvonne Ransel (https://www.facebook.com/yvonnesmusings), "but I do remember being happy that neither of them was in jail or having a baby…yet; happy that we could go on vacation without getting a house sitter; happy that I never had to go to another parent-teacher conference or sports banquet (though I did miss the actual sports/concerts/plays)."

Some parents are happy just knowing their kids are somewhat settled. Laura Ann Klein (http://www.yellowhousedays.com/) faced her share of challenges before the nest was empty. "My oldest son struggled through school, and I almost lost him to depression and addiction," she says. "My second happiness is my younger son, who's thriving in college and discovering his passion. My final piece of happiness in this empty nest is finding myself again after twenty-five years of being someone's mother—and for a good bit of that, someone's wife. Now I'm me. And I really love me," she says. Louise Cady-Fernandes (http://www.linesofbeauty.com/) agrees that when your kids are happy, it brings you an extra layer of happiness, but there's more: "The older I get, the more apparent it becomes that contentedness really begins with taking good care of ourselves, enjoying growing older, and not freaking out about it."

Sharon Hodor Greenthal (http://www.midlifeboulevard.com/) says that when it comes to happiness beyond her kids, peace of mind is key. "I don't need big adventures or lots of activity—I have found that my natural instinct, much like when I was a child, is to spend time alone, and that makes me very happy," she told me.

Laura Ehlers (http://www.coastofillinois.com/) says she's admittedly happiest on the rare occasion her family is all together, but she finds it elsewhere as well. She says, "I think it's important to *not* base your happiness only in relation to your children—or anyone for that matter. I find I can be happy when I am *in the moment* and doing things I enjoy—even if it's cleaning!"

Lisa Stapleton Weldon (http://www.lisaweldon.com/blog/) prefers trying what's new. "I find my happiness in learning again…learning social media, learning how to write, to blog. I am basking in quiet time."

For Andrea Seppinni (http://www.plantchef.com/), happiness is tied to work and exploring personal interests: "My happiness is and always was defined by and expressed through my passions. My children, though grown, still play an enormous part in how I choose to express them. When they were young, their development was my primary passion, and the additional interests, talents, or skills I had in writing—the arts and cooking, for example—were utilized for their benefit. Today, I have the opportunity to grow my passions for my benefit and share them with many people (as I have via blogging)."

Writer Mindy Klapper Trotta (http://www.relocationtheblog .blogspot.com/) thinks that ultimately, happiness is doing what you love. "Feeling creative and accomplished makes me happy, whether it's through work or writing. I am definitely happiest when I feel vital," she says.

I wrote about happiness when I was trying to decide if my sense of it had diminished, especially in the years leading up to my kids moving away. Sometimes the act of writing about a feeling or event can be quite revelatory. At first, you tell the truth as you *think* you know it, and in the manner or voice that you want to present yourself. But if you go back and edit and consider some of the deeper feelings that you hadn't let rise to the surface, *that's* when the real truth comes out. And if you're lucky, you'll find what you were looking for.

~

This week, on my way out of a restaurant after lunch with a friend—a restaurant filled with moms in their twenties and children under three, one that uses paper plates in the event a food fight erupts—I smiled and waved at a baby in a car seat perched on a table between both her parents. When she smiled back, I saw two tiny teeth poking through her drool-covered lower gums and a barrette on top of her head that cinched a tuft of hair. It was all I could do not to pull up a chair and play for the rest of the afternoon.

"She's such a beautiful baby and so happy," I said to her parents, who were watching me make silly faces at their daughter and who were clearly smitten with her themselves.

"Yes," the mom said, "and she really responds to people."

I remember those days, I thought. How fun it was to take my kids out, to watch their emerging personalities, and to be around other parents, swapping stories and making sleep-deprived adult conversation.

While I was standing there, her mom gave her a bottle. Not a bottle of the type I remembered but a new crooked shape with a nipple that looked nothing like the Playtex model of the '90s, or frankly the human model. It came out of a black bag that looked like a purse with serious insulation.

"Yeah, she's a happy handful," her mom said.

"It's a cliché, I know," I said, "but enjoy this time. It's pretty special— even the nights you're up forever and you think you'll never have a few minutes alone again. Really, it's over in the blink of an eye."

She nodded, and I thought I saw her begin to cry.

"My older son is three," she said, "and it happened so quickly. I mean, he was just born, and now he's already in preschool."

"Mine are in college," I said. "It gets harder to convince them to go places when you can't fit them into car seats with handles. There are things my husband and I said we were going to do as a family and put off because the timing wasn't right. I've learned over the years that the timing is never right when you have kids—you just have to take a leap of faith."

The baby's mother and father looked at each other, then back at me. "What else?" the dad asked. "What are some of the other things you've learned?"

I paused. He was asking me as if I knew a secret, a wisdom that is perhaps only shared at restaurants filled with parents whose kids are considerably older.

I looked outside and saw my friend standing on the corner, waiting for me to emerge. There wasn't enough time to tell them everything. And should they really hear all of it? No, they needed to discover this kind of stuff on their own. Anyway, who was I to dish out parenting advice about babies in the twenty-first century? I didn't even recognize the baby bottle they were using or the bag keeping it cold or know the latest about what position an infant should sleep in.

I looked back at the parents awaiting my reply.

"Well," I said, "there are a couple of things. The biggest is family—unless they are certifiable or criminals, try to keep your kids connected to their cousins, aunts, uncles, grandparents, whatever you've got, even if it means sacrificing vacations and that new fridge. And visit each other in good times and bad. It teaches your kids more than you can imagine about love and loyalty and means they will not only always have a place to celebrate and someone to celebrate with, but a net to catch them if they fall.

"When the kids are little, hold off on the fancy presents, even if you can afford them. It's you they want. And a cardboard box to crawl in.

"And when they're teenagers, stick around—they think they don't need you anymore, but they do, more than ever. Just try not to judge, though believe me, it will be hard.

"As for you two, don't blow it all in Vegas, but don't live to retire. Live in the moment. You never know what's around the corner."

And with that, I said good-bye.

"Who were you talking to?" my friend asked when I joined him outside.

"To the couple with the cute baby. They wanted some advice," I said.

"What kind of advice?" he asked.

"About raising kids, what I've learned."

"That didn't take long," he said.

"Exactly what I told them," I said.

~

You know how sometimes when someone asks you a question, your mind goes totally blank, and all the wisdom you've gleaned goes right out the window, and you look like a deer in the headlights? Well, thank goodness that didn't happen when I met that young family. Can you imagine how scared they'd be not only of doing the right thing by their children (the questions they asked me about), but of aging too? Personally, I was just happy to figure out that I was done with the blues and had regained my sense of self enough to share things that were potentially helpful—to pay it forward. So what about you? Hopefully, you're up and off the couch, have done some reflecting, and found tools and techniques to counter unproductive or negative feelings. Now, let's make things happen.

PART FOUR

FINDING THE RIGHT
PATH TO REINVENTION

Love and Marriage

W hen a couple marries or starts living together, I don't think
they truly know, at least for a good decade, how they're going

to fare. You can say and mean with all your heart that whatever happens, you'll make it work, but even the best-suited couples are challenged by the myriad of things life throws our way. Sometimes it all makes them stronger as a couple, and sometimes it tears them apart.

⌒

I've lived with my husband for half my life. This realization is both frightening and satisfying at the same time. If you'd asked me when I met him if I thought we'd end up here—married with two kids and living in the suburbs—the answer would've been no. It's not that I didn't want a family—there were just lots of other things on my mind at the time. My career was taking shape, I had a network of friends whose company I enjoyed, and I was finally making enough money to be able to afford to eat more than Cream of Wheat for dinner. My boyfriend (now husband) was nearly nine years older and looking to settle down. I'm still not sure it was with me, at least initially. I think he mostly had a thing for redheads, and I was sort of a redhead; if I stood in the bright sunlight, you could see red in my hair, and my skin is dotted liberally with freckles.

It took a while for us to get in sync and admit our feelings. Although I was totally into him, I wasn't quite ready to lose the apartment life (on the subway line!) I had just achieved and the freedom to make decisions that only impacted me. Having been in a terribly wrong relationship several years earlier, I was hesitant, to say the least. But love took hold, as it often does, and off we went.

By the time our children were teens, life and marriage and work had lost some of their luster, especially for me, as I thought about what the future held when the kids left for school. Between our move to Texas, Nick's childhood illness, and my own cancer, it all left me flat. When the kids did head to college, I found myself avoiding discussions and physical reminders of the past. A single glimpse of an old photo with me in it made me feel as if I was looking at a stranger—a happy, energetic, and optimistic version of myself.

Recently, when my computer died, my husband went into emergency preparedness mode. He's actually always in it—not for earthquakes and hurricanes, but for loss of historical information. Over the years, he's been the chronicler of our lives. There are the home movies from both our childhoods that he transferred to VHS, and when those became obsolete, he transferred them to DVDs that are now stored on backup drives at home and in the cloud. We have thousands of old photos that he spent days and weeks and months scanning and preserving—photos of our childhoods, our children's childhoods, his mother's and brother's child-hoods, as well as our lives together before our kids were born. Some are edited together and have been put to music; others were made into short films for milestone birthdays. Then there are the facts—every detail of business, doctors we see, accounts, major transactions. It's all noted. If there is an emergency, our records are ready to go. We have laminated emergency cards in our wallets, detailing allergies and contact informa-tion, laminated address cards with a hole punched and perfectly centered in the top where he pulls a hair band through and attaches it to luggage and backpacks. He updates these each time the kids move, which, by the way, as they're college students, is quite often. Sometimes doing all these things has kept him from being with us—as if he was not paying attention to the details of our lives.

When my computer died, he swung into action in his quiet way, setting me up in a new space with an old desktop. He'd backed up my system with two drives and loaded one of them onto the old computer. Up came my files. To make it easier for me to see, he substituted a TV as my monitor. To give me a better workspace, he pulled furniture from several rooms (we have a lot left over these days without kids at home). Then he patted my head.

I'd been looking for a childhood image of Nick and Alex when they pretended to shave with Popsicle sticks. So I reluctantly opened the archives and began scrolling through the titles. And there, in order and by date, were our lives—together and apart. It was all there, year by year, I proceeded, getting lost in it all—and much to my surprise, instead of making me depressed, it made me happy. It turns out this was one of the ways he takes care of us, of (in fact) staying involved and connected. And it reminded me of why I loved him then...and love him now.

Children do have a lot to do with how relationships change, the dynamic between two people. For some, it can be incredibly satisfying to go on the parental journey together. Sexy, even. For others, partners get jealous of the time spent with the kids. The whole who-should-come-first issue is such a personal one and so tied into our own upbringing, our perceptions of marriage and parenting, the reality of marriage and parenting, and our maternal instincts.

Over the years, I've spoken with women friends whom I've considered to be very successful in love and career, but who, it turns out, didn't always view themselves that way. And each time, it was the father/daughter relationship—or lack thereof—that they talked about affecting their self-esteem and their choice of partners the most. Given all the challenges I had with my own father, I could certainly relate.

A friend once told me she purposely avoided marrying anyone she thought might become an alcoholic like her dad. What she didn't realize was that her father had other equally serious character flaws that she didn't fully understand until she had been on her own and then married for a while. "My dad never finished high school," she said. "He joined the Marine Corps when he was nineteen and fought in the South Pacific during WWII. After the war, he worked at a Jeep factory, and at one point, he worked for the post office. Then he became a salesman for a number of companies. The alcoholism really influenced his career, and his work ethic lessened every year. I never respected him much while I was growing up, although I always knew he was funny. Then, when I attended a funeral several years ago at Arlington National Cemetery, the young marines were so elegant and strong and disciplined. For the first time, I was overwhelmed with pride for my father. At some point, he'd been one of these guys, and he tried to do what was right. Who knows what changed for him."

Another friend had a very different experience growing up. A New York City police officer, her father had never shied away from hard work. He worked his way up through the ranks, studying hard and taking written promotion exams for each level. At the same time, he attended college and was actively involved in raising his four children, one of whom had Down syndrome. When I asked her if she thought her relationship with her dad influenced her choice of mates, she said it absolutely did: "I looked for a man with principles and a sense of humor, someone who would want to make decisions with me, team up with me—all qualities I saw in my father. I witnessed my parents' loving relationship and their ability to go through life together, and that was a model for me. So it isn't just the relationship between me and my dad, but my observation of the relationship between my parents that really influenced my decision about who I wanted to marry."

Studies have shown that women do generally marry men who are like their fathers; whether they are nurturing or absent, women take their cues from the most important man in their formative years and how he treats them. Women also tend to keep quiet about difficulties at home while they were growing up. It's not that families have a conversation about doing this, but women sense that they're not supposed to tell. The result is that these girls grow up ashamed, thinking that whatever transpired was their fault—and decades later, they're in writing classes and various forms of therapy coming to terms with their feelings.

That may also be one of the many factors contributing to divorce. According to recent research, the divorce rate among people ages fifty and older has doubled in the past two decades, while overall divorce rates have declined since the 1980s. To put it in perspective, in 1990, only one in ten people who got divorced was fifty or older. Ten years later, it was around one in four—more than double. And it's largely women initiating these breakups. They aren't interested in staying in a marriage that is making them miserable. For many, the empty nest is their way out.

Just as our transition *to* parenthood had us rethinking some of our relationships, so too does transitioning away from it. Priorities shift, and along with the shift come questions.

Perhaps you're wondering if you and your partner will have enough to talk about without the kids to distract you. Or maybe you're feeling underappreciated or neglected in your relationship. Or wondering if your friendships with other moms will stand the test of time. If any of these issues ring true, you're not alone. Therapists say it's a good time to take stock of your marriage/partnership and to expand your social circle—perhaps look for mentors and friends who are doing something with their lives that you admire.

For couples, Dr. Rutherford recommends sitting down with your partner a year or so prior to the last child leaving home and asking questions such as *How are we doing? Are you happy? Do you dread the kids leaving? Are you looking forward to it?* Then, ultimately, share what you'd both like to do with your lives after they're gone. Test the waters too—on date night, make a rule: fifteen minutes to talk about the kids, then move on to other topics. The same applies to getting together with women friends.

It's all about you now—finding your path, staying the path, expanding the path. You get the gist. As you progress to an empty nest, you have the opportunity to make or deepen relationships that will enhance your new stage of life.

How to Reconnect, Emotionally and Physically

Marriage and partnerships are hard work, and over many years, issues between two people, even in the best relationships, can get swept under the rug for a variety of reasons. The thing is, once the kids leave, it's harder to avoid what you've been putting off talking about, even if it's just small stuff that's become exaggerated over time, like leaving toothpaste stuck to the sink.

There are a variety of reasons divorce among people fifty and older is on this rise, but one of the main ones might surprise you in terms of how uncomplicated it is: we're living longer. Turns out that the notion of staying together forever takes on new meaning when forever is a lot longer than it used to be. It's quite possible that your great-great-grandparents would not have remained a couple had they realized they might live longer. Or that your great-great-grandmother would not have stayed with your great-great-grandfather had there been more opportunities for her to become financially independent and divorce was more socially acceptable at the time. Since most divorces among older couples today are initiated by women, I can only surmise (and yes, interject my opinion) that one person in most marriages is the bigger communicator, and in a relationship between a man and a woman, the woman is usually that person—"the feeler," the driving force behind the tough conversations. Simply put, our generation is less tolerant of marriages that are not encouraging us to use our voices and to ultimately be happier. We divorce later in life. When the kids are gone, we've got a lot more life to live and less reason to remain in an unfulfilling marriage like some of our grandparents did.

Beyond lifespan, why do so many marriages fail? What is it that separates the good marriages from the bad? According to research by psychologist John Gottman of the Gottman Institute, one of the chief trademarks of happy couples is kindness. When you're kind, your partner feels loved, respected, and appreciated. Being overly critical keeps you from seeing the good stuff and can erode the love connection.

I asked husband-and-wife psychotherapists, relationship counselors, and authors Linda and Charlie Bloom, who have been married since 1972, if you can learn to be more kind and loving toward your partner. Their short answer was *yes*. Hold that thought. The longer answer is you should probably figure out what the underlying reasons are for not being kind in the first place, so you don't fall back into the same pattern of behavior. People who are unkind to their partner, says Charlie Bloom, "often treat themselves in unkind ways as well and project this onto their partner."

Linda Bloom says in actuality, it's hard for people to reveal their inner emotional life, so very often the conversation is only going on in their own head. "They may not be speaking it or demonstrating it in a way their partner feels it," she says. This really comes into play after the kids leave. If a couple has not been relating in an intimate way, things can deteriorate rapidly. "People tend to feel more comfortable turning toward the kids than toward their partner," she says. And if you're anger-phobic—that is, you don't like to bring up issues for fear of getting angry and making a mess—the result is that you may end up with a larger, more complicated one.

So how do you open or reopen the lines of communication in a constructive way? Talk about these concerns with your partner, and seek outside help. There are lots of resources, from community and religious-based classes and workshops to online programs, professional counselors/therapists, and relationship coaches. The main difference between counselors/therapists and relationship coaches is that counselors/therapists are licensed by the state, have to pass certain tests and requirements, and focus on helping you find solutions as well as (if appropriate) look for underlying causes for behaviors. Relationship coaches are not licensed by the state and focus on helping you find solutions. Regardless of whom you choose, the advantage of seeing a good counselor/coach or therapist, says Charlie Bloom, is that "they can see options [that] couples are otherwise blind to."

Ideally, you and your partner will work together when choosing a therapist to find someone you both like. I say ideally, because truthfully, often one of you takes the lead, at least initially. You should be able to ask the therapist questions about their experience, success rate for couples, the methods they employ, etc. Once therapy has begun, your counselor will try to help you focus on the ways in which you interact with one another—the things you say that perhaps are knee-jerk reactions, the way you do or don't pay attention to one another, criticize, judge. They can't do the work for you, but they can guide you, help you undo negative communication patterns, and try to make you aware of how you respond to your partner. The goal is to get you to focus your energy on the relationship itself so it is happier and to be more supportive of one another. If you choose to give some form of therapy a try, do it with good intentions. "You're on the same team," says Linda Bloom.

So much for talking—what about sex? What role does it play in a successful marriage after the kids leave? There are a variety of physical issues that can lead to a couple not having sex anymore, but for those not being intimate in any way, physical limitations are not usually the real cause—the quality of the relationship is. When there is an accumulation of anger and resentment, which can happen after years of putting off talking about issues when the kids are around, sexual desire is weakened. Keeping up "the love connection" is key to intimacy that lasts. And it *can* last: in a recent English Longitudinal Study of Ageing Project, researchers found that there are lots of men and women who are sexually active into their eighties. Simply kissing or touching releases endorphins and oxytocin that are "a great love cocktail," says Linda Bloom.

The study reminded me of a story my grandmother once told me about a neighbor in her retirement home. He had several women chasing after him, even though he had a longtime companion, and he was legally blind and nearly ninety. The reason? "How well he danced," she said. And by "danced," I trust she really meant danced, not something else…but maybe not. Anyway, one day, his longtime companion was supposed to be out of town and came home early and found him in bed with another woman from the retirement home, and he fell out of bed and had to go to the hospital "because things were broken."

What do men and women want from sex? The Blooms say that women report it's the high quality of the sex rather than the frequency that they seek. And for men, it's the frequency rather than the quality. Linda Bloom has found that most women are not being assertive and saying what they like, yet men want them to be direct. "Be honest, give them details…they *do* want to know," she says.

These are the nine components of healthy relationships, according to the Gottman Method for Healthy Relationships (https://www.gottman.com/about/the-gottman-method/):

1. **Build love maps:** How well do you know your partner's inner psychological world, his or her history, worries, stresses, joys, and hopes?

2. **Share fondness and admiration:** The antidote for contempt, this level focuses on the amount of affection and respect within a relationship. (To strengthen fondness and admiration, express appreciation and respect.)

3. **Turn toward:** State your needs, be aware of bids for connection, and respond to (turn toward) them. The small moments of everyday life are actually the building blocks of a relationship.

4. **The positive perspective:** The presence of a positive approach to problem solving and the success of repair attempts.

5. **Manage conflict:** "Manage" conflict rather than "resolve" conflict, because relationship conflict is natural and has functional, positive aspects. Understand that there is a critical difference between handling perpetual problems and solvable problems.

6. **Make life dreams come true:** Create an atmosphere that encourages each person to talk honestly about his or her hopes, values, convictions, and aspirations. ˜

7. **Create shared meaning:** Understand important visions, narratives, myths, and metaphors about your relationship.

8. **Trust:** This is the state that occurs when a person knows that his or her partner acts and thinks to maximize that person's best interests and benefits, not just the partner's own interests and benefits. In other words, this means, "my partner has my back and is there for me."

9. **Commitment:** This means believing (and acting on the belief) that your relationship with this person is completely your lifelong journey, for better or for worse (meaning that if it gets

worse, you will both work to improve it). It implies cherishing your partner's positive qualities and nurturing gratitude by comparing the partner favorably with real or imagined others, rather than trashing the partner by magnifying negative qualities and nurturing resentment by comparing unfavorably with real or imagined others.

Of course, there are other, more serious, reasons that partnerships don't work out, including mental health issues, substance abuse, and physical abuse. For the couples who have figured it out, so far, at least, they encourage one another to grow as individuals while maintaining their bond.

Jane Pauley has been married for thirty-four years. "I feel very happy in a nest of two," she says, "though we have created more independent than interdependent lives in our empty-nest years. Our changing work lives have been a bigger dynamic of change and will be more so in years to come."

A year or so before my sons left home, my husband and I started getting out more as a couple (rather than in a pack of four). Nothing earthshaking, mind you, but it was time alone and time away—as adults, not parents. We began to enjoy routines of our own, separate from the kids—something we hadn't done since before they were born, back when time was ours for the taking. We had to get used to just having conversations again, the way we once did, that had nothing to do with what was happening in our children's lives and us being responsible.

⌇

Let's face it—we change as we get older. Not just the obvious physical changes, but emotionally too. As we should. A lot has happened since we fell in love and had dreams of building a future with someone else. By middle age, the distance between the present and the future is a lot shorter than it used to be. We've all likely endured loss, health issues, career changes, financial issues—and marital conflict over some or all of these. Resentments over who did more child-rearing, house clean-ing, bill paying, who was more present, too absent, less tuned-in—they have a habit of festering until one day, you and your mate are standing face to face without the distractions of raising a family, and you either work through them, or you don't. Of course, therapists will tell you that working through issues as you go is the smarter way to handle things, but when life gets busy, sometimes that's not the way it really happens. Stuff just gets tabled.

There's a lot of advice out there for achieving a long and happy marriage, some of it from people who actually are in a long and happy marriage. Making time for one another, date nights, kindness, not saying "you always/never..." in an argument, fostering friendships outside the marriage—these are all cited as keys to staying betrothed.

The truth is it takes two to tango. You both have to want to keep working at a marriage. Sometimes the pain is too deep, the resentment too great. Sometimes you just plain aren't attracted in any way, shape, or form to your partner anymore.

I know my husband well. I can tell you what shoes he'll pick out to buy, the TV shows he watches, what toothpaste he uses, and that his breakfast will always be a bowl of Rice Chex mixed with Corn Flakes. But I also know there's more to him than that. I know this because there's more to me than my breakfast choices, the side I part my hair, and the color of most of my shirts (coral). After years of living in the family-focused world we created—the roles we've played thus far as parents, the way we've interacted—well, that world is no longer.

So how do I know all this? It's not therapy. It's the Corner Bakery. We've been learning about one another again over Saturday lunch at our neighborhood Corner Bakery. I order the same thing, and he likes to shake it up. We always share a dessert: whatever is new on the menu. And we take our time. Sometimes two hours or more. In the history of being us, this never happened until we started to transition to the empty nest. At first, we didn't have much to talk about other than our kids. Now we talk about everything and nothing at all. Sometimes we read the paper.

We're still here, together, because we want to be. And though we're married to each other, neither of us is married to the way we've always done things.

So we're starting over again, except this time, with the foundation of a shared history. This wasn't a conscious decision, starting over—it's more of a naturally unraveling one. Our kids are only home for holidays and summers. Unfinished conversations we had when they were little have stayed unfinished, not because we're avoiding them, but because they're no longer relevant. What's relevant to this relationship is where we go from here. How we treat one another going forward as a couple with dreams that are still unfolding.

As of last weekend, we're at twenty-four Saturdays and counting.

~

Okay, what if you're married to someone you love but feel you are no longer *in love* with? Whether it's a question of kindness, intimacy, physical attraction, or maybe your relationship has just lost something along the way—can you get it back? Again, the short answer is *yes*. When someone says this (*I'm no longer in love with my spouse*), Linda Bloom hears something different: "What I hear is that they miss that aliveness and intensity…but we see evidence that it's possible [to get it back]." It's often quite a bit of work to do, she says, because the magnetism has drifted away, but that doesn't mean that good feelings aren't still there waiting to be reignited.

It's all about intention—showing that you want things to work out, that there could be more to the relationship that wasn't possible before. Winifred White Neisser says that after the kids left, she and her husband were alone in the house saying, "Who are you again? Now what do we do?" It didn't take that long for them to adjust and to recognize that they could be a lot more spontaneous than they had been:

> On Saturday afternoon, we could decide, *Let's go to the movies tonight*. We had just stopped doing all that stuff and instead were making sure we knew where the kids were and how they fit into the equation. I was thirty-six when I got married. My husband and I were only married a year before our first child was born. We had no married life where it was just the two of us. I think that was a concern that I was afraid to articulate: *What if we find out now that all we had in common was raising our kids? What if we can't figure out how to have fun just the two of us?* Fortunately, that wasn't the case.

The Blooms say that by the time a couple comes in for help, an average of six years has passed since they began having problems, and many are having serious difficulties. That, says Charlie

Bloom, is why so many people give marriage counseling a bad rap. "They've waited so long, it creates new related problems—there's just a huge backlog of problems, and by the time they get into therapy...when the kids leave home, they are...like psychic strangers." He's quick to add that everyone has some marriage issues, by the way. They know one another well because they have lived together for so long, but really, in many senses, they're strangers to one another emotionally.

Create a plan or agreement for how to discuss things when and if they do get too tough to handle on your own, but do it long before they reach that point—like when things are peachy. A *We'll be together forever and everything you do is perfect, but if we ever start getting angry at one another, let's go to a therapist or promise to watch the movie* Moonstruck *while eating oysters and making out* sort of plan.

The Blooms created a marriage agreement of sorts themselves and have, on occasion, exercised it. Linda Bloom says it has given her great peace of mind over these many years because it helps her avoid conflict—you only need to remind one another of the agreement, and go get help. Sometimes "three heads are better than two," she says.

As for actually broaching the topic of therapy when you don't have a previous agreement about going? Honesty is the best policy. And if you want to give it a try and your partner doesn't, go yourself and do your own work. "If he sees really positive changes in you," Linda Bloom says, "maybe he'll join in at some point, or do the work on his own."

To begin a dialogue and to get a better sense of your empathy skills as a couple, try asking each other these three basic relationship questions. If the outcomes are not what they should be or could be, talk it through. If you still have issues, perhaps it's a good time to find some help.

1. When I have good news, my partner (a) acknowledges the news and is supportive, (b) doesn't acknowledge the news, (c) brings up how difficult it will be to follow through on whatever the news is—i.e., paying for the master's program you just got accepted to.

2. When I express my needs, my partner (a) does not acknowledge them, (b) makes me feel badly for bringing them up, (c) listens carefully and discusses them.

3. My partner (a) has my back, (b) does not have my back, (c) has no idea what having my back means.

One of the biggest fears I've heard women express was what would happen to their partnership/marriage when the kids left. Journalist Michele Willens says she was happy to discover that her own fears were unfounded: "My husband walks around saying, *What's the bad side of the empty nest again?*" As for the concept that marriage post-empty nest should be compared to marriage before the kids come along—that is, exciting and full of life—she says, "Exciting is not fair…what do you think is going to happen?"

Not everyone wants excitement—at least not at first. Writer Sara Parriott says it's taken her and her husband a while to want to do something more than chill. After raising two children, one of whom has special needs, and then helping her mom for years, they are gradually adding new things into their days that are just for them. "We're trying to find a rhythm," she says. "It's taken a while." One of the most rewarding things for them now is seeing their son become independent. "It's like a miracle," she says.

Risa Nye says she and her husband are quite happy to be "back to two" and got great advice about marriage from a friend:

> Someone told us many years ago to plan one night for *us* alone—put the kids to bed and have a nice dinner, even if you don't sit down until nine o'clock or ten o'clock at night. We did that for years, finally going out when the kids got old enough to leave at home. Because of that, we didn't find a stranger at the other end of the table (or on the other side of the bed) when the kids left. For a while, I felt a little bereft. Although we were both working when our youngest left, I was the one who came home to an empty house, so I think I felt it a little more. We never really had big noisy fights or anything, but with no kids around, we can be more candid with each other and not worry about who's listening at the top of the stairs. I should add that we've been together since 1969—with no breakups or separations—so we have a long history to look back on. We were a married couple for nearly five years before our first child came along, so we remember what it was like. We're more focused on *us* now, although we keep an eye on what each kid is up to. It's been a gradual shift to *our* future, as opposed to theirs, which I think is a good thing. We still keep our bedroom door closed, but I don't really know why!

Beth Havey (http://www.boomerhighway.org/) emphasizes the importance of common interests and mutual support:

> We have been the best of friends for forty-four years in marriage and for fifty-one years if you include dating. We still share the same faith, the same politics, and of course our

children and grandchildren are amazing familial bonds. Our love, every aspect of it, is still present and giving our lives joy. Though my husband has been through a lot with his chronic illness, even after a day of chemo, he would get up the next morning and go to work... He is strong and forward think-ing, and that helped me to believe and be strong. Maybe some people don't realize that every day of family life, you are building toward the end of that family life. If you love and give and support, it most probably will come back to you when you need it. And believe me, we all will.

For Kay Williams, a fifty-six-year-old working mom of three, when her kids started leaving for college, she says it became increas-ingly difficult for her and her husband of twenty-five years to find common ground, and their marriage deteriorated. "I had a sense that it was happening for a while, long before I actually admitted it to myself," she says. "It's easy to hide behind kids...or let your family be a buffer. But my husband and I did fewer and fewer things together. And it just wasn't there anymore."

The couple discussed marriage counseling, but they had different perspectives. "When you still love someone, but he doesn't want to go to counseling or figure out how to be aligned again, it's left to you," she told me. "Deciding between the slow private desperation of feeling yourself becoming someone that you don't recognize and watching your husband become someone that you don't recognize either, versus the emotional train wreck of a divorce in which there are so many other casualties—people you love, not just yourself—it was a wrenching decision."

To help her figure things out, Kay often turned to women friends, many of whom were uncomfortable discussing divorce on any level. "Women I've known for years shut down and didn't want to talk about it," she says. "It's almost like it's contagious, as if it would make them think about their own life and see potential cracks in the foundations of their own seemingly solid relationships."

In the end, she decided to ask for a divorce.

Kay and her husband still share their home. She lives downstairs, and he lives up. The kids come over frequently, and they hang out and watch movies or fix meals together now and again. "It's becoming less painful over time," she says. Together, they're finding their way to a friendship based on what they've shared—it's a new layer of their relationship. "I'm surprised how many people think that it has to be more adversarial, but it's our story, and that's how it's rolling out."

Friendships

Women and their friends are the subject of tabloids, books, movies, and, well…women. Some of those friendships take root early in life, some later; regardless, they're all impactful in one way or another. As we move through the various stages of parenting, we often find ourselves surrounded by the same group of women, sometimes intentionally, sometimes just because our children are friends. It wasn't until after my sons went off to college that I started to get to know some of these women on a more personal level. I think it's because we finally had time to talk.

~

When my sons were little, there was a group of moms I talked to at school functions and basketball games, mostly about our kids. Now, the kids aren't the reason we socialize—we do it because we want to.

There are seven of us—from different parts of the country, with different backgrounds, different interests. Our get-togethers began right after our kids headed off for their freshman year of college, and we decided to meet for dinner. As the wine started flowing, we shared stories about the transition to our new stage of life, and it didn't take long before we realized that a recurring if not unexpected theme had emerged from conversations with our sons—laundry. Yes, that's right; the few phone calls we'd received from them during those early weeks away were neither emotional nor deep but were mostly filled with questions and concerns about doing laundry:

"Can I wash the blue sheets with the white towels?"

"This washing machine opens from the front. Is that normal?"

"The sign says you have to use cold water. Can I use it for my whites?"

"How much goes into a large load?"

"Mom, seriously, this is going to cost a lot of money."

It's not as if the guys had never done laundry before. It's just that they had never done it without a backup within earshot. And clearly, as a result, they never actually paid attention to what we were telling them until they were staring at several large loads of dirty laundry with a line of other kids behind them.

By the time dinner was over, the moms had vowed to meet once a month or so, either at a restaurant or each other's homes. Then we named ourselves the Motherload, in honor of the load of laundry questions directed at us.

Each time we get together, we unravel a little more about ourselves— about who we were before our kids were born and, most importantly, where we're headed now that they're off to school.

Last night, the Motherload spent the evening in a newly designed space. It was the former living room of one of our more artistic members, who had transformed it into a post-empty-nest wine-tasting room (because the old space, she said, only gathered dust). The decorative wall art formed from cement, bricks, and stone framed by delicate ironwork; the table that became the centerpiece; the elegant sideboard—they were all crafted by her and her husband, who, in spite of the fact that they both work, are enjoying some downtime now that the kids live away from home.

We'd all brought something to eat, and since everyone is health-conscious but not opposed to the occasional sweet, we mixed hummus and artichoke dip with mini Kit Kat bars on the same plate (or maybe that was just me). While we ate, we talked about our health, our changing careers, the classes some of us are taking, how some of us no longer make our beds every day, our kids—how we grew up versus how they did, and about the challenges of being a young parent today versus when we were young parents. We also talked about the benefits of the Internet and mom blogs, resources we wished we'd had when the lists of questions about parenting were long and libraries were closed in the middle of the night.

Eventually, the evening came to an end, as all good evenings must. We said our good-byes and planned to meet again—many of us have challenges ahead that might delay but won't deter our get-togethers, because we know that nothing replaces a real, live, in-person community of moms.

When my kids were little, I rarely did this—spent time alone with other moms. I was always too busy, or tired, or rolled my eyes at whatever I thought was the stereotypical "mom" event. *I'm different from them,* I thought. *I don't need that kind of bonding or support.* But I was wrong. Flat-out wrong.

To every mom out there: Don't just embrace the online community. Get out and connect in person as well. Meet when you can, even if only a few times a year, without the kids. And yes, I know, just because someone is a mom doesn't mean you have lots in common. But over time, you may discover that there's more to that other mom than you ever knew—that she is not perfect, that she does not expect you to be perfect, and that you might be surprised to learn that she eats mini Kit Kat bars with artichoke dip, just like you.

~

There's a body of research, says Dr. Irene S. Levine, a friendship expert, author, and journalist, which links friendships and social support with improved health, happiness, and longevity. My maternal grandmother lived to age 107, and I do believe that the friendships she made added years to her lifespan. She was a role model. It wasn't that she had a big career or solved all the world's problems—she didn't. But she did make an enormous impact on her family and friends with her generous spirit.

When Nana moved to a retirement community, her life

reminded me of my college sons'—her friendships, her meal plan, the way the neighbors kept their doors open half the time and came in and out of each other's apartments, even the way they traveled in groups and talked about who liked whom. There were laundry rooms at the end of each hall, and the machines took quarters. There were also issues with who was sitting at what table for lunch (I guess that part never changes), and tables that seemed to be reserved for the people she thought were mean girls and horny boys (for the record, I lived for those stories), but Nana made the most of the opportunities for developing friendships and living life to the fullest every day. Even when she had to stop doing certain activities, she never altered her perspective. And she was genuinely happy—it was contagious. I often asked her how she coped when her friends passed away; Nana outlived all her siblings, all her peers, and most of her relatives. She told me she made sure to wake up each day with something to do and someone to look forward to doing it with. That the journey of life is far more rewarding with friends to share it with.

During your transition, some of the friendships you once held so dear may not stick. It can be surprising to learn who you are really most compatible with, and not because anyone has done anything wrong, but because your needs have changed—your goals have changed. That can be a hard thing to talk about. I recently had a friend call me out on the distance I'd been keeping from her and our larger circle of friends. I knew she had noticed but was giving me space. I also knew she'd bring it up—carefully, but directly, and when we were alone. That's why she's a keeper. She's tuned in and honest and funny.

So what makes a good friend? Loyalty and trustworthiness,

for starters—and they should show an interest in you, take the initiative to plan things (this can often end up being one-sided, and eventually, that person gets weary and resentful). You also want someone who is your equal in terms of how you live your life and treat others—but it's not about the size of your house or your income (though those things can make it hard to feel a balance in the relationship). It should also be someone who is interesting to you and has qualities you admire. How many friends you have "is a matter of choice," says Dr. Levine and varies for every individual. Some people prefer one close confidant and more downtime alone; others enjoy multiple friends and derive energy from the heightened level of activity that comes with them.

If you were to take an objective look at your friends, who inspires you the most? Makes you laugh? Is there a particular personality you attract and who is attracted to you? All things to consider when you are in transition. "My best friends include fellow nursery and kindergarten moms and dads from twenty-five years ago!" says Jane Pauley. "I have a best friend from work going on nearly forty years. I've made new friends through new work in the last decade and even the last year. And I credit my husband for keeping old friends in active circulation. But I mostly owe my friendships to the luck of being attached to women who won't let me succumb to a tendency to social inertia. Staying connected doesn't come naturally. My mother's dearest and only friends were her two sisters. I'm blessed with a very close sister bond, but it's not enough."

"Old friends, I swear, are in your bloodstream, your bones," says Beth Havey. She continues:

They are the golden oldies. My Chicago friends who were there while raising my daughters and my Des Moines friends who were there while raising my son are still in my heart. We email. Some visit. My husband and I go to their children's weddings when we can. It's a process, as everyone has busy lives. But certain ones are always there for me, and they are the oldest and dearest, the ones from the very beginning. Friends are precious. Since we moved, I only have a few in the new community, and when you don't have children to pull you into groups of people, it takes a lot longer. And I guess I'm more content to write and read, though I did join a book club. I confess, I miss my friends from Chicago and Iowa. That's why social networking is nice. Not the same, but helpful.

When talking about friends, I don't mean to exclude men, by the way. Some of my closest friends are men. On the subject of women and men being friends, psychologist Levine says it's all fine and good as long as there are no mixed messages. Sometimes one person has romantic feelings and the other doesn't, and in those cases, you do need to talk about things—make sure you're both on the same page. It's also important that your partner is okay with the friendship and is not threatened by it in any way.

One of the best fixes for a mom in transition is hosting a group of friends where you don't focus on making things perfect but on the friends themselves. Mine your childhood for some inspiration for things to do that make you feel like a kid again and that don't involve talking about your own kids. I'm just saying, Mad Libs are still out there. Scrabble too.

Breaking Up

What about when a friendship goes sour? What should you do? As people change and move in new directions, we often find our friendships do too. Sometimes it can be very painful, "especially," says Levine, "if the decision to break up is unilateral." Often, you don't know why the friendship ended. In these instances, it generally has more to do with the other person's life than something you did or did not do. Levine says there's frequently a secret that they didn't feel they could tell you—a difficult relationship issue, an illness, or a perception on their part that they are not equals in some way. Closure in these cases may not be possible, as difficult as that may be.

Other times, it may be more apparent, like something you said or forgot. These things you can address quickly, apologize for, and hopefully your friendship can move forward, depending on how your apology is received. If, on the other hand, you see a pattern in the way you are treated—that is, your friend disappears frequently, blows up, makes a scene, etc.—you may need to let the friendship go. Unlike a marriage contract, where you take vows and should work on issues, the rules for friendships "are much more cloudy and ambiguous," says Levine. Regardless, don't ever let yourself say something you might regret. That friendship may be resurrected years later.

Writer Candy Schulman's (http://www.candyschulman.com/) friendship with a woman she'd known for years couldn't have been more perfectly scripted. They related emotionally and intellectually, were both parents, city dwellers, and genuinely enjoyed each other's company. Then, one day, something changed, and Schulman was left standing alone, wondering what had happened and when.

I met Diane on a school tour when our kids were four. We were both passionate about foreign films, gourmet cooking, and politics. I thought we'd be friends for life. She joked about how we'd live together in our old age.

Her son and my daughter never really clicked, but Diane aggressively fostered a fifteen-year friendship with me, often calling every day to talk about issues ranging from school to a controversial newspaper article. We bought each other's kids birthday presents, melded our families every Thanksgiving for a feast, and comforted each other when I needed shoulder surgery and her brother tragically died.

The first year our kids went to college, she'd call and say, "It's our new life! Let's meet for coffee," or "Come take a long walk with me—it's a beautiful afternoon." The next summer, she suddenly grew distant. I kept asking if something was wrong, and she'd respond, "No, just busy." If I asked her to get together, she'd email back, "Sorry—busy." I asked again if something was wrong. She said no. After a dozen "Sorry—busy" responses, I just stopped trying. That was six months ago—I haven't heard from her since.

We live in the same neighborhood, and I know we're going to run into each other eventually. What will I say? Will I try to get her to explain why she pushed me away and inexplicably severed our friendship after fifteen years? I'll probably just smile and say hello, then quickly go on my way.

I too had a story like this that involved a woman I considered to be one of my dearest friends. We met when our firstborns were toddlers and knew one another when we were pregnant with our second children. In spite of the many ways we were different—our backgrounds, especially—we still clicked. We spent time alone together, as well as time with our families. There were dinners and sleepovers with the kids that involved movies and made-up games that left us all laughing until it was time for bed. We knew one another's extended families too, frequently celebrating birthdays together. Then my family moved away, and soon after, I was diagnosed with cancer. I heard from her maybe twice, only after my treatment was done. Although we were no longer in the same state, there were many opportunities to connect. I got the message, whether it was intentional or not, that the effort was more than she wanted to make. I think about it and mourn the loss still.

Reaching Out

When we're little, our friends are, in fact, the people we are surrounded by: the kids at school, in our neighborhood, at religious events, in sports and extracurricular activities. We sometimes simply need to say, *Will you be my friend?* And it's as easy as that.

We'd just moved halfway across the country when my oldest son was about to start middle school. Although the goal was to try to help our children meet other kids before the school year began (and he did), the first week of school was still the stuff of YA books about being the "new kid." The cafeteria, like most middle schools, was chaotic to say the least. And everyone, old and new, found new seats at tables and sorted themselves out eventually—the cool kids, the jocks, the brilliant kids, the mean girls... One afternoon, soon after he started, I asked my son how it was going—how he was feeling about the people he met and if he saw some potential friendships unfolding. His answer surprised me in how thoughtful it was. He said it was so much easier for girls to make new friends, that he didn't mean to be offensive to girls, but it seemed like they could say things like I like your headband or I like science too, and that's it—boom, they were friends. Guys, he said, aren't like that. Not that they are deep or anything, he went on, but they have to find friends differently. Sometimes it's more what they do or how they rib one another. Someone at the table he was sitting at made him laugh so hard that milk came out of his nose, and after that, he and everyone around him (who also enjoyed laughing so hard that milk came out of their noses), began a friendship then and there, and they are still friends a decade later.

So if you like milk, there's always that...

As we mature and develop our understanding of what being someone's friend really means, we start to seek out companions with shared interests, sensibilities, and backgrounds. By the time we have our own family, we often find ourselves connecting with other moms whom we see regularly through our children. To say these friendships are born out of convenience isn't quite fair, though in many respects, it is an easy and obvious fit—you're a mom, she's a mom, you're around one another a lot and can support one another, and you share similar experiences at this stage of life. But truthfully, it's more than likely a mix of factors that made you take the leap of faith and start a conversation to begin with. These types of friendships can be lifesavers, from carpooling and babysitting to meals, advice, and finding someone to laugh and cry with.

But what if being a parent with kids in the same community is where the connection begins and ends? What then? Levine says the more you have in common with someone, the better chance you have of making a friendship last. So if you haven't had the time to do things with your mom friends outside of events that revolve around the kids, now that you do have more time, give it a try. Plan a get-to-know-the-*other*-me lunch or dinner, where you go around the table and talk about things that are separate and apart from being a mom. Are there goals or dreams you put on hold? Hobbies you might share but didn't realize you did?

Mom-of-two Josann McGibbon says that after her kids went to college, she made a "conscious decision" to see if women friends wanted to do things like having coffee. Writer J. D. Rothman says she too finally had more time to spend with some of her longtime friends and is still very much connected to many of them today. In fact, she really misses the soccer moms. They are like her long-lost relatives: "If I hear from them, I'm really happy."

To expand your circle of friends beyond moms, psychologist Barbara Greenberg suggests you try new things and create "an updated version of yourself." The bonus is meeting people with shared interests. Here are a few ideas, from the more traditional to a few you might not have considered:

- Take your dog to a dog park.
- Get involved in a community program.
- Start a meet-up group.
- Sign up with your local nursery for a workshop on how to grow a garden or vegetables.
- Volunteer at a local library, church, hospital, or cancer center.
- Join a book club.
- Join a group that takes walks or hikes or cycles.
- Join a knitting group—they often meet in libraries or at yarn shops.

- Sign up for special events like food and wine tastings.
- Arrange a dinner where each of your friends brings a friend you haven't met.
- Attend author events at your local bookstore.
- Attend a conference or convention related to your work, interests, or hobbies.
- Start a journaling group—simply writing down the highlights of your life and sharing some of them can be validating.

The idea is to get out of your comfort zone and shake it up a bit. Start a conversation that you can continue over time. Speaking of conversations, beginning one with a stranger can be as awkward as being on a first date. Dr. Greenberg says that to break the ice, be as natural as possible, inquiring about the person's routine in whatever new activity you share. Ask *What's your normal exercise routine? What kind of meditation do you do? Do you have a garden?* Then, very gradually, move on to other topics: *What are your favorite books? Movies?* There should be a back and forth.

Complimenting someone is always a good conversation starter, as long as you're doing it in a sincere way. "The idea is to show an interest, but not too intensely," says Dr. Levine. "You don't want to come off as too needy." Not everyone is looking for new friendships.

If you know you have similar interests, live in the same neighborhood, are involved in the same civic groups, go to the same gym, etc., ask about her experiences in these environments "and find the commonalities between you," says Levine. You're more likely to make friends with someone you know on some level, which is why if you can put yourself out there—try new things and then let those friendships happen gradually—it will feel more authentic. It's easier to make a friendship out of an acquaintance, says Levine, than a stranger.

Lisa Carpenter has had great success meeting friends using social media. "I've made many new friends as an empty nester, most of whom I met online, then the friendship moved into a face-to-face stage. Some categorize their connections as IRL (in real life) versus online, but to me, online *is* IRL these days, and many of my friendships forged online have become deeper and more satisfying and supportive than those with some of the folks I knew offline first," she says.

Of course, not all attempts at friendships work. I once impulsively struck up a conversation with a woman whom I regularly see sitting alone at my local coffee shop. I told her she looked like she belonged at a café in Paris, that she smelled amazing (really, she did), and I asked about her brand of perfume. In retrospect, that was pretty dorky of me and probably sounded like I was about to ask her on a date. Plus, I forget that I am only fashionable in my mind when I go out to get caffeine, because I'm usually wearing my "writing clothes"—which is to say, I look less than fabulous. She, on the other hand, always looked *truly* fabulous and was always dressed for a *Vogue* photo shoot. Well, turns out she didn't just look French, she *was* French. That's when she started to tell me in broken English/French (I think—I had almost no idea what she was actually saying) about her perfume, going so far as to try and draw me a picture of the bottle because she could not recall the name of it. This (also in retrospect) should have been a clue about what was to come. After our initial conversation, she never recognized me again. Ever. Or didn't want to. I prefer not to know which. I do, however, recognize her (hard not to—her scent leaves a trail), and yes, she still sits alone. But whenever I see her, I'm reminded that I tried, and that means I'm making progress. Right?

If you're in a relationship that isn't making you feel good about yourself and find that you're giving more than you're getting back, then it's time to reevaluate it. From your partnership/marriage to your friendships, if you need an objective opinion and guidance, consider a relationship coach, a therapist, or a counselor. As we age and our children move on to their own busy lives, the people we choose to surround ourselves with become even more important. It's always a good time to establish new friendships, especially with people you admire and respect. They're an investment in our future and can bring balance and laughter to even the most mundane aspects of our day. Remember: in any relationship, kindness and generosity are key to its success.

Passions and Careers

When I was in my twenties and living in New York, I kept a diary. It was hard not to: there were so many things about my life that were new—people I met, places I went—and I had to put it all somewhere. After I moved away a few years later, I ditched it and didn't resume writing anything similar until I was diagnosed with cancer in my forties. Then, when my treatment ended, so too did the diary. The empty-nest series on *Huffington Post* was my updated equivalent, with the difference being that this time, I wanted to share it. The writing was a way to connect to other women in the same stage of life. Also, it was a lot cheaper than therapy. I hoped the series would lead to a book, and then eventually to more books on additional topics. I say hoped, because I know from professional experience that these things are always a long shot—and that they take time. I also knew I finally *had* more time and needed to use it well (after all, I wasn't in my twenties anymore, and I *was* a cancer survivor). That's not to say I woke up each day and wrote from dusk to dawn. I didn't. And there were certainly days when I forgot how determined I was. But never for long—especially after I discovered Starbucks' hot green tea and pumpkin bread, which I admit to using as a reward system when I complete certain goals…or sometimes to be able to complete certain goals. It all depends on how you look at it.

When our children were little, I asked my employer about the option of more flexible hours. It was a relatively novel idea at the time, so I wasn't surprised when the answer was no—disappointed, yes, but not surprised. So I made the difficult decision to leave and go freelance. Difficult because so much of my identity was tied to my work, and I enjoyed the camaraderie, the creative environment, and the income.

Now, years later, I don't have regrets, but I do have other thoughts on the topic, especially as it relates to what's best for a woman down the road when the kids are grown. In my case, I figured I'd deal with whatever the obstacles to reentering the full-time workforce were when the time came. I'd do whatever needed to be done to make it happen. This make-it-happen attitude is the trademark of many moms, and we use it regularly on behalf of our children. But when it comes to *us*, especially at this stage of life, we often forget how to be our own best cheering section.

Today, as I consider full-time work again, work/life balance is still an issue but for different reasons. After years of juggling freelance work with family needs, I prefer to stay the master of my own schedule. I'm pretty good at it. That, and the working world really does favor young people in full-time job searches, though as the mother of two such young people who write, I've got to say, the compensation is not exactly painting a pretty picture for doing what you love and expecting to support yourself at the same time.

The topic of working moms can be polarizing. Regardless of whether you do or don't have a career while raising a family, the decision to work is a personal one and varies widely by circumstance and values.

While Sara Parriott's kids were growing up, she found her niche writing feature films with her writing partner, Josann McGibbon. This success eventually made her the primary income-earner in her marriage and helped her son receive the special care he needed. She and Josann scheduled their work so that they could drop off and pick up their children from school. It wasn't always easy, and they were grateful they had this flexibility, but it came at a cost: they lost professional opportunities for more lucrative and prestigious writing jobs in television that involved very intensive and late-night schedules.

Eventually, after the kids were on their own, they were able to "ramp up" and take on the challenge of writing for television. It's something they had always wanted to do, and they've loved doing it. Now, some fifteen years later, the partners find themselves at a point in their lives when they are wondering *What's next?* Is it time to "ramp down"?

Whether you're hoping to start a career for the first time, shift careers, or reenter the workforce after a long hiatus, you'll need to chart a course and come up with a plan to get there.

If you've been thinking you're too old to begin something new, science is out to prove you wrong. Turns out that the expression "you can't teach an old dog new tricks" is no longer relevant. Our brain is constantly adapting and changing, which means there is no magic age at which you stop learning. In fact, it's quite the opposite. When we have new experiences, not only can we learn from them, but we're also retraining our brains. As we challenge ourselves and acquire new skills, the brain rewires and remodels itself.

What, exactly, will your new challenges be? And how should you begin your job search? Nancy Collamer, a career coach, speaker, and author of *Second-Act Careers: 50+ Ways to Profit From Your Passions During Semi-Retirement*, says that when she meets with moms who are looking to return to the workforce or change the course of their careers, she starts by talking about blocks. Yes, blocks—the plain, wooden blocks that young children use to build whatever comes to mind. She says these blocks are a great metaphor for appreciating the diversity of your skills. Just as a child continually assembles these blocks into new forms (a castle, a barn), you too can use the skills you've gained in both your professional and personal life as building blocks for a wide variety of careers.

Mary Dell Harrington, cofounder with Lisa Heffernan of the blog *Grown and Flown* (http://www.grownandflown.com/), shifted her life's work several times as her children were growing up and continues to do so. The two moms began the blog when their youngest kids were in their junior year of high school and say it's been "incredibly satisfying work." Some of what Harrington does now for the site relates back to her previous career in media at NBC and Lifetime, "but in a creative, entrepreneurial, and infinitely more flexible way," she notes. "I realize that I'm substituting potential financial rewards in favor of creativity and flexibility, but I'm happy with that trade-off." Harrington also began taking writing lessons around the same time and says that in retrospect, she took baby steps: "I wish I'd been more focused on relaunching with a career in writing sooner."

Skills. You need them to do any job. If you had a previous career and took a hiatus to raise your family, you're in a wonderful position to do what many people who've worked continuously don't often get a chance to—reconsider your career path. Perhaps the path was intentional, or maybe it's a job where one thing led to another. Regardless, you're here now, at a crossroads, and can decide what direction you'd like to explore. What skills did you employ in your career that you enjoyed the most? Liked the least? Make a list.

Think about the skills you developed as a mom. After all, you weren't born a mother. Here are some examples:

- As a parent, did you spend time creating and organizing school events or extracurricular programs? You may be a natural at event planning.

- Were you managing multiple projects as a volunteer and at home, including budgeting and working with other people? Perhaps you'd make a good project manager or volunteer coordinator.

- Do you/did you have a child who requires special care? You may know more about medical insurance, billing, or caregiving than the average person. This could translate into a future career in the medical or insurance fields.

- Were you the parent who made the desserts that everyone raved about? Maybe there's a career in baking in your future.

- Are you a whiz at computers and computer programs? You might be interested in an IT career.

- What about politics? Did you campaign for change at the local level? Perhaps there's more for you to do in your community and beyond.

You get the gist. Here are some additional professions that might be a natural outgrowth of your raising a family:

- college advisor
- interior designer
- photographer
- professional organizer
- legal professional
- accountant
- travel agent
- writer
- CEO
- speaker
- communications manager
- publisher
- chef
- insurance agent
- teacher/tutor

That's not to say you don't or won't need more training and education in a given field, but if you have the aptitude *and* a desire to pursue your talent, you're on your way. Before I left my full-time work to begin a freelance career, I made a list of my own skills. It's always a reality check when you have to be objective about yourself and your abilities, then figure out how those skills translate to real jobs.

Of the skills I noted, three came up repeatedly: conceptualize, manage, write. Next, I considered how I might utilize these skills in a freelance capacity and if there was a market for them. To get a sense of how to update my résumé for freelance work, I took a look at the competition using online job banks. Since the trade association

I worked for represented the food industry, I narrowed the focus of my search to food and health. I also researched what it meant to be a freelancer from a contract, tax, and insurance perspective and found a few organizations online (there were a lot fewer then) where I was able to get freelance rates along with copies of contracts that I adapted and made my own. This included everything from individual jobs, to monthly and yearly contracts, to those that related to hiring video crews. Finally, I spoke to a few key people (some of whom had previously expressed interest in my working for them as a freelancer) about my upcoming plans and my time frame for making the switch. In the interim, I printed business cards, set up an office at home, and completed a few small writing gigs. Around a year after I first began researching the idea, I left my full-time work with a freelance contract in hand. More contract work followed.

What about interests? How can you uncover what you might be overlooking? Collamer suggests you dig a little deeper than the obvious by answering these questions: *What did you most enjoy doing as a child? Why?* If you liked to draw, for example, and then said the reason you liked to was because it gave you a sense of calm, you felt creative, and you could do it alone, then you may be best suited to work as a freelancer in a field where you can incorporate drawing—anything from design to architecture to construction. The goal in your search is to not only uncover your natural skills, but also your interests and working style. As we have all come to learn, just because we're good at something doesn't mean we can see ourselves doing it long-term as a career. Other questions Collamer suggests you answer: *If you could make a documentary about any subject, what would you choose and why?* And *If you won the lottery and never had to work again, how would you spend your time?*

Assessment tests can be helpful if you're still struggling with what work you think you're best suited for. You can find them online and through career coaches (see below). Although skills are what employers pay for, Collamer cautions that they're not enough. The job needs to interest you in some way. Sometimes you don't have a choice—you need a job, and you take it, period. But if you can blend your talent with an interest and/or your personal values, you're more likely to stick with it and be eager to wake up and go to work. In a nutshell, if the employer makes plastic balls, are you okay with talking about plastic balls all day? Whatever the focus is, you *will* be talking about it. All. Day.

Career counselors and coaches can also help you narrow down your skills and interests as well as offer a variety of services for a variety of industries, from résumé writing and helping you create a LinkedIn profile to uncovering your dream job over many sessions. Some people call themselves coaches but are actually résumé writers, while others do assessments. Be sure you are clear with them about what you want and need. Collamer advises that you ask them to spell out what the deliverables are, along with the cost. Rates vary widely and can start around $100 an hour for career coaching to thousands of dollars. Some coaches say they need a minimum of three months, and some say more. As for résumés, they can run from around $200 for a simple one-pager to as high as $5,000 for a complete executive branding package, which can include a LinkedIn profile, cover letter, executive summary, and several different versions of your résumé. The bottom line is this: while these services can be helpful, the industry is large and unregulated and can feel, says Collamer, "like the wild, wild West." Referrals are often the best way to find someone. Be sure to narrow down the counselor or coach's area of expertise: Is it helping moms get back to work? Working with executives? Do your research.

To stay relevant, you not only need to keep honing your skills—you need to be open to change. And it's not just for the obvious reasons of wanting to be valued by employers. It's because the more you know, the better you feel. You're the only person with your particular experience and background. That makes you unique. I think women are the first to forget this. It all comes back to investing in yourself in some way. Of feeling worthy. To put it in financial terms, if you were paid for being a mom, what salary (on average) do you think you'd receive? In 2014, www.salary.com looked at the top ten jobs that moms (most, not all) are responsible for doing, then broke them down by hours and number of days per week spent on them. The result? If you were paid for being a mom, you'd make over $118,000 per year.

Although she worked throughout their childhoods, when J. D. Rothman's kids went to school, she took on more. That's when she noticed that the majority of the people in the meetings she would attend were under thirty years old. On one such occasion, it occurred to her that she had worked with a female executive's mother, and that she had, in fact, babysat the now-grown executive while her mother was on a business trip. One of those moments, no doubt, when you not only need a sense of humor but to quickly refocus on the skills and knowledge you bring to the table (babysitting not being one of them). Rothman spent many years juggling work and parenting. In the end, she's glad she did. "There's something to be said for earning money for what you do," she says, while acknowledging the constant philosophical divide. "Work gives you structure, money, self-worth." Her advice to other moms looking to start or relaunch a career? If you've done lots of volunteering, try to use that as a springboard for consulting/freelance work that you can get paid for. Or try to volunteer somewhere that might lead to something where you get paid. And "get exercise," she adds. "The endorphins make us less depressed!"

What about gaps in your résumé? A pro can spot time lapses quickly. The good news is that you *can* take steps to close the gaps by taking classes, doing freelance work (paid and unpaid), volunteering, and interning. Yes, interning. It's not just for college kids, and more and more often, it's a paying gig. Following are more details on how education, freelancing, interning, and volunteering can be effective gap-fillers and résumé-boosters.

Education

Returning to school doesn't necessarily mean getting a four-year degree. In many cases, a program that certifies you in a specific area is the golden ticket. For these programs, begin your search with your local college. "Community colleges are underappreciated resources," Collamer says. Not only do they offer affordable career courses, but they often take it a step further, working with community leaders to determine what local businesses and services are understaffed and in demand. For example, a nearby hospital may have a shortage of technicians in a variety of areas, then approach a community college about the challenge of attracting and training a workforce. The college will then provide programs to help fill that need. There's also a Plus-50 initiative (http://plus50.aacc.nche.edu/) by the American Association of Community Colleges where, in addition to courses, community colleges offer career counseling and networking programs for people over fifty hoping to get back into or change careers. So get on the mailing list for your local college and look over their course catalog. "You might stumble on an area you didn't even realize interested you," says Collamer.

Many technical schools and industry associations also offer certificate programs, another great option. And don't forget recreation centers—they host low-cost courses that can help you get up to speed on such topics as budgeting and social media. If you need help with undergraduate, graduate, online, and career schools, try www .petersons.com. For free online college courses, try www.coursera .org. Keep in mind that the drawback with online courses versus on-site courses is that you don't have the same opportunity to meet new people and network. That said, you need to have options that fit your lifestyle, and if online courses are all you can do for now, take them and find other ways to network. Before you spend the time and money to enroll in anything, see what industries are hot and hiring at the Bureau of Labor Statistics website: http://www.bls .gov/bls/industry.htm.

Motherhood came late in life for journalist Michele Willens, who had her second child when she was forty-three. She loved the experience. So much so, she was concerned about *not* having a child at home. "The kids were always my priority," she says. When her youngest was in high school, Willens says she felt "unfinished" and decided to try and go back to school part-time. She had taken classes previously at a local college, but this time, she wanted to be enrolled in a regular degree program, so she went through the application process, wrote essays, the whole thing—and had to wait to learn if she was accepted, just like any college-aged kid. "It was really hard," she says. "I do everything late in life... But I always said [school] was in preparation for the empty nest." She was accepted to Columbia, where she takes a couple of classes at a time. Over the years, although Willens remained a journalist, she's tried other forms of writing as well, including playwriting. Some of the projects she's taken on have been interesting experiences, but ultimately, she found some of them too stressful to continue. It's important to accept the truth, she says. As for her concern about the looming empty nest? "My fears were unfounded," Willens says. She's happy being busy and productive and creative. "An active life is key."

Five years after her youngest went off to college, Risa Nye left her career as a college counselor and entered an MFA program in creative writing. "Since then, I've been a freelance writer, with two regular gigs that pay me and one volunteer job that doesn't."

Freelancing

Don't be afraid to use your personal connections to network your way into a job, including reaching out to contacts you made through previous work. Collamer suggests that you offer to do a project for someone for free or a low fee in exchange for building a portfolio and having a reference. Some online job sites, like www.flexjobs.com, charge a small fee but specialize in freelance listings. They also have a large library of articles you can access.

Interning

As we discussed, these are a great way to make connections that can lead to regular employment. Most large companies have internship opportunities and list them on their websites, Facebook pages, and Twitter. Follow their posts for the most up-to-date information. Some are paid, and some offer college credit—many follow school schedules and last for a semester or the summer.

Volunteering

Offering to work for free can sometimes lead to a regular job, though it's not necessarily at the place you're volunteering. Sometimes it's the result of the networking you're doing while volunteering—the people you meet along the way. "At a minimum," says Collamer, "you're doing something that adds value to an organization." You're also building your skills and filling gaps in your résumé as you go. Make sure you're spending your time wisely though and working at a company that is involved in your career interest. See http://encore.org, www.volunteermatch.org, www.idealist.org, and www.irelaunch.com for listings.

Job Search and Résumé Tools

If you've ever done an online job search, you've found that there are zillions of job boards online. Some charge fees, and some don't. Find the ones that specialize in the areas you're interested in, then create a profile. You'll get updates (as frequently as you choose) on job openings. You may also get mailbox solicitations for résumé writing services and more, so be sure to carefully check and uncheck boxes before you submit anything. And don't forget about temp agencies. They're not only still around, but they offer a variety of types of jobs that go way beyond the administrative work that you might recall from twenty-five years ago. Some even look for CFOs, CEOs, and senior marketing executives. Career placement services are also an option. Again, make sure you know exactly what they will help with and what their fees are. If you've already graduated (recently or long ago), your college's alumni or career services department may be able to help as well.

What if you've found a position but aren't sure it's the right one for you? Here are some points to consider:

1. **Work culture**—Do you prefer a smaller, more personal work environment, or a large one? Does the company promote from within? Is there an emphasis on team building? How diverse is the workforce? Are there cubicles? One large, open space? Can you work from home if need be? Is there flextime?

2. **Lifestyle**—Are you okay with a one-hour commute? Do you need to dress up? Travel? Bring your lunch? Is this a job you can see yourself doing at sixty-five? (Don't think short-term—many people today are working well into their seventies.)

3. **Values**—Is it important to you that the work be meaningful and fulfilling? (If you're in a financial position where your salary is not as important as the work itself, this may be a larger consideration in your search.) Does the work conflict with your value system?

While her kids were growing up, Winifred White Neisser worked full-time. She was with NBC for many years as vice president of family programming, director of movies for television, and vice president of television movies, then moved to Sony to become senior vice president of movies, television, and miniseries. Being a mom and an executive always left her with this nagging feeling that something was "left undone," either at work or at home. A few years before her youngest went off to school, she knew she wanted to make a career change. After her son graduated from high school, she applied for and was admitted to a graduate program at Harvard— the Advanced Leadership Initiative. The program is essentially for people of retirement age who have been leaders in their fields and who want to make an impact on society in a way that perhaps they couldn't during their careers. The change has been a big one for Neisser, moving from the home she shares with her husband of more than twenty-six years to her own small apartment near campus until her coursework is complete. "It's interesting living by myself," she says with a laugh. "I talk to my husband every day, but I was really nervous about it. Now, I almost feel guilty about how much I like it." Still, she admits that's likely because she knows there's an end date in sight—that she'll be back home soon.

For now, she loves the stimulation of being on a university campus: "There are lots of things I'm interested in and get excited about the way I haven't been in a long time." When she's done, Neisser hopes to work for a nonprofit and have some flexibility so she can continue to try new things and visit her kids, who are just beginning their own careers and likely won't have the opportunity to travel home.

What woman do you admire most? Is she someone you know, someone in the news? What is it about her that stands out? Her business acumen, attitude, boldness, creativity? From here on out, think of her as your role model. In every situation related to your career search, ask yourself how that person might handle things. What would *she* do? While you're at it, toss in some of that enthusiasm and energy you reserved for your child over these many years and sprinkle it over yourself like fairy dust. And whatever happens in your career search, don't give up. Not even when you're met with *no's*—or worse, without any reply at all. When and if you find yourself losing momentum, channel your role model and tell yourself that it's all just part of the process. Here are some additional ways to get the help you need, especially if you're returning to work after a long break:

- **iRelaunch** (http://www.irelaunch.com/) is a resource for career reentry: they have an extensive and targeted list of career reentry programs (including internships) and also events, coaching groups, and success stories. Their annual Return to Work Conference is a large-scale gathering of returning professionals (primarily women) and the employers interested in hiring them.

- **The Transition Network** (http://www.thetransitionnetwork.org/) is a national nonprofit that supports professional women over fifty who are in transition (that's you!). With chapters around the country, TTN connects women through transition peer group meetings, special interest groups, programs, and events that explore a variety of topics including finding your next career, launching a business, or discovering your own "what's next."

- **Life Reimagined** (https://lifereimagined.aarp.org/) is a service made up of tools and community to help people reflect, evaluate priorities, and take action to live their best life. Accessed both online and offline, the Life Reimagined experience offers a personalized, step-by-step approach to help people discover new possibilities, guide and prepare them for the change they want, and support them as they make it happen.

- **Next Avenue** (http://www.nextavenue.org/) is a website for people fifty-plus. Public media's first and only national service for America's booming older population, their mission is to meet the needs and unleash the potential of older Americans through the power of media.

Carol Fishman Cohen, a mom of four, CEO and cofounder of iRelaunch, and coauthor of *Back on the Career Track: A Guide for Stay-at-Home Moms Who Want to Return to Work*, says that if you're a mom who is hoping to return to the workforce, in addition to identifying what you want to do before you begin a search, be sure to reconnect with people from your past. "Even if you're afraid that it's been too long," Cohen says, "reach out." LinkedIn is great for this. You can go to their resources section and follow the free online tutorial to figure out how to set up your profile. LinkedIn offers you a low-key way to get back in touch. Once you do, ask if your connection can give you fifteen to twenty minutes of their time for a phone call. Cohen says to tell them upfront that you're not calling about a job, but in essence, "you're going through a thoughtful process to determine where you can add the most value, now, to an employer. Ask if they can walk you through changes that have occurred in your industry over the last ten years while you've been out of the workforce."

Another approach, she says, is to ask them to share their career path. Did they leave and go to work for the competition? Switch industries? Start their own company? "Tell them this could be helpful to you in your own thought process as you are figuring out what you want to do," she says. Tell them "that you're in information gathering mode." People are often hesitant to reach out to old contacts, certain that they won't reply. But Cohen says that's not the case; more often than not, they do reply, and the results (she has seen them) are very positive. There is no downside to trying.

Regardless of how accomplished you were in your career, if you took a break from it to focus on family, your sense of self can, over time, take a hit. To build up your confidence, Cohen, who returned to the workforce after eleven years away, says to keep these two thoughts in mind:

- When you get back in touch with people from your past, people with whom you worked or went to school, they remember you as you *were*; they have a *frozen-in-time* view of you. So though *your* sense of self may have diminished over time, *their* view of you has not changed, and it is a great confidence boost to hear their enthusiasm about your interest in returning to work.

- Once you figure out exactly what you want to do, have conversations with your nonjudgmental family and friends to rehearse your story. The more times you tell it and get solid feedback about what you're saying, the better you can express it. You'll soon excel at talking up your interests, and when you do, you'll not only feel more confident but project that confidence.

After her twin sons went to college, Georgette Adrienne Lopez set about reinventing herself. With a law degree that she wasn't using and financial issues to work through after a divorce and job changes, it took her a while, but with the help of unwavering friendships, Lopez rebuilt her life, step by step. She drew from her previous experience as a television producer, using her skills coaching talk show hosts before they went on the air, and redirected those skills toward herself for job interviews. It worked. After selling her house, finding a job that she enjoys, and moving into an apartment, Lopez is feeling more in control of her future. The bonus is having time to spend with her adult children. "I've become a new type of mom," she says, one who she wasn't able to imagine a few short years ago when dropping her sons off at college.

Columnist Beverly Beckham says that although "your kids are your passion, you need another one." Today, in addition to her journalism career, she's taking singing lessons. Growing up in a house with a mom who sang was part of her inspiration. That and the fact that when you're older, you tend to interpret courage differently. To Beckham, "courage comes when you look at the clock, and tick tock." When she sings, it makes her stop thinking, and all the "bad stuff" goes away. Beckham says her new approach is to take things one day at a time—to "live in the now."

An Inspiring Story of Rediscovery

Mithra Ballesteros has four sons and blogs at www.thebubblejoy .com. When her oldest son left for college, it was a tough adjust-ment, and she grew depressed. "I spent a good year," she says, "thinking long and hard about how to move forward. I would watch the show *Girls* and marvel at the irony that I had so much in common with those young, lost souls." As the oldest in her group of friends and the oldest child in her family, Ballesteros didn't think she could talk about it to anyone, that anyone would understand. "I felt I had no right to be upset...it seemed shallow and selfish, and I was ashamed of feeling this way," she says. Her mother was her role model, having raised four children as well. She seemed, says Ballesteros, to have moved with ease and joy into her next stage of life: "In so many ways, that was part of why I was so ashamed."

When Ballesteros' third son went to school—he was a loving caregiver for her youngest, who has special needs—she was hit hard. Luckily, she had taken a part-time job when her oldest left a few years before, and through the job, she was able to continue making gradual, thoughtful changes: "That introduced people into my circle who knew nothing about my kids and my family."

When she came home, Ballesteros says she could share things

about her day that had nothing to do with her children, and it gave her a better sense of herself, which also helped her children to see her in a new light. With this confidence, she was able to look at some of her friendships more objectively, and at that point, she says, she made some decisions to "start surrounding myself with women I admired." She also began therapy and started writing again. That's when she understood that above all else, she needed to keep writing, that it was part of who she was and who she wanted to be in her newly emerged form: "I needed to find something I was good at besides being a mother."

The whole process of rediscovery for Ballesteros took around a year; then she took another year to start writing posts. Today, with the help and encouragement of her husband, she has an online business (http://www.findernotkeeper.com/) where, as a "collection creator and a storyteller," she finds and matches interesting collectibles for people who appreciate their individuality but who don't have the time to do it themselves. Then she blogs about the process. She refers to her work as instant pop-up collections of arts and antiques for walls and tabletops. "It's wonderful to feel like I have a purpose," she says, "and that I'm good at something and valuable to society beyond raising four sons. I see my friends with younger kids who are now struggling the way I was." She says many of them are encouraged by family to go get a job—that they feel this pressure to do something, because women today are inundated with role models on social media, and then we look at our mothers and how some of them aged, and she says we are trying to figure out what we want: "We feel guilty a lot."

After years of raising her kids and thinking she was resilient and positive, it turns out she grew less and less so every year. It all makes her wonder if women who work throughout raising their kids are better situated after the kids leave: "I contend that I paid a price by staying home with my kids. Aside from giving up earning potential and inadvertently enforcing negative stereotypes about women, I set myself up for a harder transition post-child-rearing—it's a hidden cost." Still, she says, "I was the one who made the choice and know that I was fortunate to have the choice." It wasn't easy though. With four sons, one of whom has learning disabilities, "our life was chaotic at the best of times—it was all-encompassing, 24/7." She took a rather large leap of faith to try and start her own business—and her kids are very proud of her. As is she. "Because I changed the trajectory of my own path," she says, "I think my children are better men."

Pay It Forward

Many of the women who are featured in this book took the time to consider the type of work they wanted to transition to before their children left home. Some were dealing with aging parents, health issues, divorce, financial issues, and more. But they took steps to keep themselves moving at whatever pace they could. Once you've taken a few steps of your own, reach out and share your experience with the mom who is expressing concern about where her future will lead. Or maybe the one who isn't, who seems to be holding back, afraid she's the only one having difficulty with the transition. Tell her what you've done and how you've done it. Share your sources and resources. Pay it forward—it's the single best gift any mom can give another mom. It's wisdom born of success, failure, grit, and most importantly, love. iRelaunch would love to hear from you too—visit their website to post your story.

Transformation: Me, Reinvented

After one long year of preparation and change, I finally understood what I had to do, how to do it, and that I was capable of
following through.

~

They're coming home for Thanksgiving in search of homemade meals, a
warm bed, and sleep. So I've been thinking...maybe I could leave town
for a while?

I love my two kids with all my heart. It's just that while they were
away for a few months and going through roller coaster changes, I've
been going through a few of my own. And they haven't a clue. Why
should they? They're focused on becoming the adult versions of
themselves—learning, growing, thinking more independently, becoming
more independent. That's why they're in school. To them, I'm Mom, and
I'm always here, in this house, being a mom.

But what if, while my sons have been away, I rediscovered some of
the things I used to like to do but haven't had time to do until now?
What if, while they've been away, I considered some new roles and new
career paths?

What if I discovered that I enjoy having less responsibility? Does that
make me a bad mother?

My house looks different, runs differently. I buy laundry detergent in
the small size, cook meals that last for several days, eat breakfast sitting
down—and sometimes that breakfast consists of one big cookie and a
cup of hot tea.

My closets and drawers reflect the biggest change. The things inside
them that sat on shelves for years—that I looked at but never really noticed
anymore—suddenly became very noticeable. The kids' grade-school

projects, papers, study guides, pencils, markers, notebooks, etc. I finally sorted through them. The old student directories, the PTA cards—I tossed them out. Well, most of them. I saved a few for memories' sake. I even went through my sock drawer and got rid of the ugly, worn ones. The old me would have just moved the socks to the laundry room to use as dusters. But not this time. This time, I threw them away.

Now, I'm wondering how many plates two people really need and what else I can part with that I once thought I could never part with.

The exercise machine that was gathering dust has gone to a family with three boys. I've reclaimed as my own the space it once occupied. My camera, once my favorite means of expressing myself, is back in business. Over the years, it had become more of a tool to document life and had lost its luster.

As for schedules, well, I don't know what homework or paper is due or when. There are no books to run out and buy at 9:00 p.m. for a class the next day. The list of to-do's has gone from spiral-notebook-size to little-sticky-size.

I do still receive emails from the kids' old high school about volunteer opportunities. I'm not ready to delete myself from that list quite yet. It's all too new, this idea that they don't live here full-time anymore.

Last night, my husband and I watched a movie about a French chef, and I remembered that I forgot to go to France. And Nova Scotia, and Alaska, and pretty much everywhere.

And now the kids are coming home, and I've missed them, and our family unit, and the way they call my name. But I've missed me too. And I didn't realize how much until they went away and I emptied closets and drawers, making way for new memories, new things that I may toss in a few more years.

So what if, when they come home, I'm a different mother? The same

loving mom, but different perhaps in other ways? I know they'll be different young men. Will we still connect? Will we fall into old roles or ease
our way into new ones? Have I learned anything over these many years?

It wasn't just the kids coming home that was making me question
everything—I was also feeling the effects of turning an age I never
imagined I'd be. I mean, really, I look in the mirror and I keep expecting
to see my eighteen-year-old self staring back.

I decided to make a nonscientific and totally biased list of my accumu-
lated knowledge. It came out in somewhat fortune-cookie language—
with advice.

1.   **Sleep is overrated.** We make way more time for it than we
     do for living our dreams. As someone said, you can sleep in
     the grave.

2.   **Sex is not love.** It just seems like it at the time.

3.   **Love is not sex.** It just seemed like it at the time.

4.   **We don't own our children.** We shape them and introduce
     them to the world—then we set them free.

5.   **Shit really does happen.** Sometimes for days or weeks or
     years in a row. You have to believe it will come to an end, or it
     never does.

6.   **Cars are not toys.** Regardless of how fun they seem.

7.   **Mothers are imperfect.** Commit this to memory if you want a
     better relationship with your own.

8.   **Some days are better spent staying home and watching
     movies.** The real world will still be waiting the next day, and a
     break from it can be a good thing.

9.   **Cooking Brussels sprouts will make your house smell.**
     When you cook them, a neighbor you haven't seen in a long
     time will ring your doorbell.

10. **Men are instinctive, but not when it comes to knowing what a woman needs.** You have to spell it out, and not enough women do.

11. **The way a man treats his mother is a sneak peek at how he might treat his girlfriend or wife.** This is not science, just long-term observation.

12. **The way a man treats his daughter directly affects her self-esteem.** This is not science, just long-term (and personal) observation.

13. **You have to keep reinventing yourself.** The world is constantly changing, and unless we do too, we become obsolete.

14. **Make lists.** They show intent. And somehow, magically, things get done.

15. **Show up.** It shows intent. And somehow, magically, things happen.

16. **Don't be afraid.** It's wasted energy that you could expend doing something, which keeps you from being afraid.

17. **Believe in yourself.** No one else will if you won't.

18. **Rethink endings.** When you think you've reached one, make it a middle instead.

19. **If you have kids and see them off to college or a career, be proud.** Then remember number eighteen.

In the end (or the beginning, depending on your perspective), when the kids returned for break, we didn't fall into old roles. That's mostly because I accepted that our new universe began with me, and I had to take the lead. Between my book project and regular freelance work, I knew that not only could I *not* be all things to all people, let alone myself, but I no longer wanted to be. I felt a little guilty, I have to admit. But when I said out loud (that part was hard for me to do) that I was swamped and loved them but couldn't stop working to do all the things they had grown up seeing me do and...you know the end of this story, right? They were like, "Uh...okay." And they helped make meals, went to the store and got groceries for all of us, or ate whatever they could find in the back of the fridge. And here's the kicker: we planned activities around all of our schedules, not just theirs. The bonus was that they began to ask me about my work and how it was going. It's as if the light in every room in the house changed, and we all saw one another differently. Let's be honest—I saw myself differently.

Because You're Worth It

About those big questions I asked at the very beginning—I decided to answer some of them in my very last blog for the *Huffington Post* series.

~

Here we are, one year later, and I've graduated to Act III. All in all, during this process, I've learned a lot about the importance of letting go, moving forward, sitting still, and the many benefits of friendships and a career.

The house—do I stay or do I leave?

I couldn't get over the idea of living in a house without kids. Why would anyone want to live in a house without kids? Of course, that is what people do. It's just that when you take away what was always in that house— the energy and love that comes with raising a family—it's awfully quiet. Memories are triggered by the simplest things: a light switch, a hallway, a smudge on the wall. So when both my sons were away at school, all I could think about was how much I wanted to move—how much I needed to move.

Over many months and return visits home by the kids, that sense of urgency began to wane. The memories became a good thing, not a painful reminder of what once was. Here, in this house, this home, there is a place for them still—a place for all of us to reconnect. At some point soon enough, that will change, but for now, as we continue to adjust to our new lives—the kids especially, as they move from dorm to dorm, apartment to apartment—it seems there really is "no place like home."

My career—what's next?

Let's face it, raising a family takes time. It's a job, and a very important one. When I left my full-time work to go freelance, it was so that I could be present for my family in a way that was important to me. Along the way, my freelance career changed focus. Now, all these years later, I am, as always, considering a number of different paths, working on a number of projects. The difference is, I can focus more on me. It's taken some getting used to, this shift in focus. It's more about permission. About giving myself permission to do what I need to do to stay relevant and engaged. To feel creative again.

For many moms, this is the hardest part of Act III—finding the confidence, the drive, to focus on themselves, to be their own best cheerleader. And I can tell you this: it's not a quick process, but it's the key to everything. You have got to believe in yourself.

If food is love, how do I adjust from cooking and shopping for four to cooking and shopping for two?

It's my upbringing. I can't help it. Food is love, and when the kids are home, trips to the grocery store are to buy foods that not only nourish their bodies and minds but their hearts. I want them to feel loved, even if it's with a bowl of pasta. Now that they're away, not only has my food budget been slashed, and my husband sometimes does the grocery shopping, but I'm less stressed about mealtime. Let's just say that I no longer count bananas. Or care if I run out of something. It's not unusual for us to eat breakfast for dinner or to skip it altogether and eat cheese and crackers and something green to relieve the guilt. Sometimes, when my husband is away, I forget the guilt and eat a slice of my favorite cake for dinner along with a glass of milk. When we both really want to feel loved, we go out to eat. It's liberating not to be the main link in the food chain anymore.

Who does the chores?

The biggest secret I learned after the kids moved away is that chores are highly overrated. Now, they get done when I feel like it. The things that once drove me batty, that seemed to be about teens ignoring parents and their requests, drive me batty no more. There is no yelling. No dividing chores up. My husband and I live simply. Quietly. And surprise of all surprises—the world has not yet ended because laundry is still in the laundry basket. Just don't tell the kids.

Will I date my husband again?

Parents making time for one another while raising a family is not an easy thing to do. The cost of a babysitter, coupled with the actual cost of doing whatever you decide to do, can be prohibitive, let alone finding the energy after a long day. My husband and I missed a few thousand dates along the way, and I worried about what might happen when we didn't have the kids around to focus on. But time has a way of healing all wounds if you let it, and conversation, common interests, and a shared history go a long way as well. So yes, I'd say we're dating again. Getting to know the new, old us, after more than two decades.

Will I become a couch potato?

I used to hate the idea of sitting on a couch. There was much too much to do to sit still, and sitting still is unhealthy besides. Now that the kids are gone, I understand that it was partly all that, yes, but mostly, there just wasn't a place for me. Now, I have a couch of my own. And in moderation, like everything else in life, it turns out it's not only quite healthy to sit still but downright pleasant. And I've earned the right.

What about travel to faraway places?

It's on the list. But with two kids in schools on opposite coasts, that's a lot of expensive airline tickets in and of itself. Still, I'm starting to let myself dream. Paris is looking mighty fine.

It's been twelve months, and I've got a while to go yet. There are issues to be resolved, questions to answer. Making friends unrelated to being a parent is tops on my new list. So too is being a part of my children's adult lives, but from a wholly different perspective—one where I'm connected in a meaningful way, but not the same way I once was. I'm here for the asking, but I'm asking less and less of them and more of me.

No, I still don't have the laundry room I always wanted, but I do dance to Al Green when I fold clothes. Nor do I have the good set of knives and the enamel pot I was going to buy for the last twenty years. Somehow, roasts were made, cucumbers were sliced paper thin, and onions finely diced.

As for time, I'm learning to measure it day to day without the framework of raising children. It turns out they really do return for school breaks, and when they do, those pantry wall measurements for every inch they grow are still being added.

They go away, yes. But not forever. Just for longer and longer. Transitioning to their absence is about shifting the focus, allowing yourself to reevaluate your own needs, hopes, and dreams, finding love, reconnecting.

~

You too are either on the verge of or already transitioning to a new stage of parenting, of looking at yourself and your life differently, of measuring your worth in a whole new way. Regardless of where you are in the process, you feel something. Something big. And you're not alone.

Do you remember the L'Oréal hair-color commercial (first aired in 1971) that launched the catchphrase "Because I'm worth it"? The slogan was written by a woman copywriter who was only twenty-three years old at the time. It was a revolutionary concept— the idea that you, a woman, were worth investing in. As a young girl, I remember listening to conversations that moms were having about its meaning and then hearing the phrase used by multiple generations, over several decades. I found myself reciting the line aloud at numerous points in my life—a reminder, of sorts, of what I didn't always let myself believe. "Because I'm worth it"—that will never go out of style. Commit it to memory, and use it as a reminder that you're worthwhile.

If you find yourself questioning the choices you made in the past, remember, it's good to question; it means we're paying attention. But we must not dwell. That only leads to regret, and as we learned from Dr. Margaret Rutherford, that's a dark hole you don't want to fall into. Next time you find yourself doing this, employ the techniques we've discussed and remove the judgment from your thought process. Make whatever it is you're thinking about an observation, not a criticism of yourself. It's not about what you didn't do that matters; it's about where you go from here. And you'll never get anywhere if you beat yourself up. In fact, if you haven't already, go ahead and make that list of skills we talked about earlier in the chapter. Next, add your favorite personal accomplishments. If you think it's your kids, so be it. List how you think you helped them become your favorite accomplishments. Are you a good teacher? Listener? Toss in what makes you feel happy. Is it reading? Helping others? Eating chocolate? Solving puzzles? These are all clues to you—the real you, waiting to take center stage.

So start the transition early, preferably when your kids are in high school. If time has slipped away and you're already staring at an empty nest, there's always today. Think about who you are, how you want to grow personally and professionally, and the kinds of friends you want to take with you on your journey. And focus on the long term. Remember that the plans you make today will take you through the second half of your life. You may want and need to be working at age seventy. There's no reason to be miserable doing that work. Your transition is a chance to reboot. You may now be in a position where other people's schedules don't impact yours like they used to. That can open up all kinds of possibilities. Don't forget to seek out mentors and role models. And stay focused on you.

As I sit down to write this, my oldest son is rethinking his career path—wondering if his college major will lead him where he thought he wanted to go. We've been talking a lot about dreams lately—about his dreams for the future, what he wants to do with the rest of his life—and I want to fly to school and make him dinner and pat his head and tell him it will all work out, to just give it time and keep moving forward. But I can't. Instead, I listen, ask questions, and remind him how capable he is. Encourage him to follow his instincts and seek out his role models for advice. I talk to him about courage and outlook and resilience, about the bonds of friendship, the benefits of an education and networking. The more I do this, I'm struck by how much his transition and that of other soon-to-be-graduating college kids is not unlike my own transition and that of other soon-to-be empty nesters. It makes me feel both young and old at the same time. Old, because I am the sum of my life's experiences, which, by virtue of my age, are many. Young, because in spite of my age, I suddenly feel free to try new things the way I once did. It's the best-kept secret ever—that you have more than one crack at designing your future, and that each step you take along the way informs the subsequent ones.

Blend the suggestions included here with your own personality and vision. And much like the old spin art at state fairs—where you pick your paints and then stand back and watch as the machine swirls your colors onto a canvas—just know that when it all shakes out, you will have art. And that art will be one of a kind.

If I had to condense this book into one sentence, here's what I'd say:

The empty nest isn't really empty unless you let it be.

RESOURCES

These websites and blogs can help provide valuable information and support to you during your transition to the empty nest. Happy trails!

AARP http://www.aarp.org/

Mithra Ballesteros http://www.thebubblejoy.com/

Beverly Beckham http://www.bostonglobe.com/contributors/bbeckham

Better After 50 http://betterafter50.com/

Karen Blessing http://www.bakinginatornado.com/

Linda and Charlie Bloom http://www.bloomwork.com/home.html

Brené Brown https://www.ted.com/speakers/brene_brown

Louise Cady-Fernandes http://www.linesofbeauty.com/

Lisa Carpenter http://www.grandmasbriefs.com/

Club Mid http://www.scarymommy.com/category/club-mid/

Carol Fishman Cohen http://www.irelaunch.com/

Nancy Collamer http://www.mylifestylecareer.com/

Coursera https://www.coursera.org/

Laura Ehlers http://www.coastofillinois.com/

Encore.org http://encore.org/

Entrepreneur.com http://www.entrepreneur.com/article/245953

Flexjobs http://www.flexjobs.com/

The Friendship Blog http://www.thefriendshipblog.com/

Becky Galli http://rebeccafayesmithgalli.com/

The Gottman Institute https://www.gottman.com/about/

Dr. Barbara Greenberg http://drbarbaragreenberg.com/

Sharon Hodor Greenthal http://www.midlifeboulevard.com/

Mary Dell Harrington http://grownandflown.com/

Dr. Jennifer L. Hartstein http://www.drjen.com/

Beth Havey http://www.boomerhighway.org/

Lisa Heffernan http://grownandflown.com/

Lois Hoffman http://www.happyselfpublisher.com/

Huffington Post http://www.huffingtonpost.com/50/ and http://www
.huffingtonpost.com/parents/

Idealist http://www.idealist.org/

iRelaunch http://www.irelaunch.com/

Laura Ann Klein http://yellowhousedays.com/author/lauraaklein

Dr. Irene S. Levine http://www.thefriendshipblog.com/

Life Reimagined http://lifereimagined.aarp.org/

Danyelle Smith Little http://www.thecubiclechick.com/

Doreen McGettigan http://www.doreenmcgettigan.com/

Midlife Boulevard http://www.midlifeboulevard.com/

New York Times http://well.blogs.nytimes.com/category/family/?_r=0

Next Avenue http://www.nextavenue.org/

Risa Nye http://www.risanye.com/

Peterson's http://www.petersons.com/

Dr. Carl Pickhardt http://www.carlpickhardt.com/

Plus 50 http://plus50.aacc.nche.edu/Pages/Default.aspx

Psychology Today https://www.psychologytoday.com/

Yvonne Ransel https://www.facebook.com/yvonnesmusings

J. D. Rothman http://theneuroticparent.com/

Dr. Margaret Rutherford http://drmargaretrutherford.com/

Scary Mommy http://www.scarymommy.com/

Candy Schulman http://candyschulman.com/

Andrea Seppinni http://www.plantchef.com/

Janine Talbot http://www.momofmanywords.com/

The Transition Network https://www.thetransitionnetwork.org/

Mindy Klapper Trotta http://www.relocationtheblog.blogspot.com/

UCLA Mindful Awareness Research Center http://www.marc.ucla.edu/

VolunteerMatch.org http://www.volunteermatch.org/

Washington Post https://www.washingtonpost.com/lifestyle/on-parenting/

Lisa Stapleton Weldon http://www.lisaweldon.com/blog/

SOURCES

A variety of materials were used to help research and write this book, including:

Books

Cohen, Carol Fishman, and Vivian Steir Rabin. *Back on the Career Track: A Guide for Stay-at-Home Moms Who Want to Return to Work*. New York: Hachette Book Group, 2007.

Davidson, Richard J., with Sharon Begley. *The Emotional Life of Your Brain: How Its Unique Patterns Affect the Way You Think, Feel, and Live—and How You Can Change Them*. New York: Plume, 2012.

Grosz, Stephen. *The Examined Life: How We Lose and Find Ourselves*. New York: W. W. Norton & Company, 2013.

Leider, Richard J., and Alan M. Webber. *Life Reimagined: Discovering Your New Life Possibilities*. San Francisco: Berrett-Koehler Publishers, 2013.

Articles

American Pet Products Association. "2013–2014 APPA National Pet Owners Survey Statistics: Pet Ownership & Annual Expenses."

http://www.petfoodindustry.com/articles/3515-appa-releases-2013-14
-national-pet-owners-survey.

Beckham, Beverly. "I Was the Sun, the Kids Were My Planets." *Boston Globe*,
August 27, 2006. http://www.boston.com/news/local/articles/2006/08/27/
i_was_the_sun_the_kids_were_my_planets/.

Blow, Charles M. "The Passion of Parenting." *New York Times*, November 6,
2013. http://www.nytimes.com/2013/11/07/opinion/blow-the-passion
-of-parenting.html.

Brown, Susan L., and I-Fen Lin. "The Gray Divorce Revolution: Rising Divorce
among Middle-Aged and Older Adults, 1990–2010." March 2013.
https://www.bgsu.edu/content/dam/BGSU/college-of-arts-and-sciences
/NCFMR/documents/Lin/The-Gray-Divorce.pdf.

Garrett, Mario D. "Brain Plasticity in Older Adults." *Psychology Today*,
April 27, 2013. https://www.psychologytoday.com/blog/iage/201304
/brain-plasticity-in-older-adults.

Henig, Robin Marantz. "Why Are So Many People in Their 20s Taking So
Long to Grow Up?" *New York Times*, August 18, 2010. http://www
.nytimes.com/2010/08/22/magazine/22Adulthood-t.html?pagewanted
=all&_r=0.

Lee, David, James Nazroo, Daryl O'Connor, Margaret Blake, and Neil Pendleton.
"Sexual Heath and Well-Being among Older Men and Women in
England: Findings from the English Longitudinal Study of Ageing."
January 2015. http://www.elsa-project.ac.uk/publicationDetails/id/7548.

Montenegro, Xenia P. "The Divorce Experience: A Study of Divorce at
Midlife and Beyond." *AARP The Magazine*, May 2004. http://assets
.aarp.org/rgcenter/general/divorce.pdf.

Oregon State University. "No More 'Empty Nest': Middle-Aged Adults
Face Pressure on Both Sides." January 25, 2013. http://oregonstate
.edu/ua/ncs/archives/2013/jan/no-more-%25E2%2580%259Cempty

-nest%25E2%2580%259D-middle-aged-adults-face-family-pressure
-both-sides.

Picha, Tracy. "Stalking the Meditating Brain." *Mindful*, August 2014. Print Edition.

Pickhardt, Carl E. "Adolescence and Revisionist Parents." *Psychology Today*, June 11, 2012. https://www.psychologytoday.com/blog/surviving-your-childs-adolescence/201206/adolescence-and-revisionist-parents.

Roberts, Sam. "Divorce After 50 Grows More Common." *New York Times*, September 20, 2013. http://www.nytimes.com/2013/09/22/fashion/weddings/divorce-after-50-grows-more-common.html?_r=0.

Salary.com. "14th Annual Mom Salary Survey." Accessed February 1, 2015. http://www.salary.com/mom-paycheck/.

Schwandt, Hannes. "Unmet Aspirations as an Explanation for the Age U-shape in Human Wellbeing." CEP Discussion Paper No 1229, July 2013. http://cep.lse.ac.uk/pubs/download/dp1229.pdf.

Shipman, Claire, Shipman, Katty, & Shipman, Kay. "The Confidence Gap." *Atlantic*, May 2014. http://www.theatlantic.com/magazine/archive/2014/05/the-confidence-gap/359815/.

Smith, Emily Esfahani. "Masters of Love." *Atlantic*, June 12, 2014. http://www.theatlantic.com/health/archive/2014/06/happily-ever-after/372573/.

Thomas, Susan Gregory. "The Gray Divorcés." *Wall Street Journal*, March 3, 2012. http://www.wsj.com/articles/SB10001424052970203753704577255230471480276.

United States Census Bureau. "Current Population Reports: Projections of the Number of Households and Families in the United States: 1995 to 2010." April 1996. http://www.census.gov/prod/1/pop/p25-1129.pdf.

Vespa, Jonathan, Jamie M. Lewis, and Rose M. Kreider. "America's Families and Living Arrangements: 2012." August 2013. https://www.census.gov/prod/2013pubs/p20-570.pdf.

Wudarczyk, Olga A., Brian D. Earp, Adam Guastella, and Julian Savulescu. "Could Intranasal Oxytocin Be Used to Enhance Relationships?" 2013. http://www.ncbi.nlm.nih.gov/pmc/articles/PMC3935449/.

Websites

http://www.bloomwork.com/

http://www.carlpickhardt.com/

http://www.cdc.gov/

http://www.drmargaretrutherford.com/

http://www.thefriendshipblog.com/

https://www.gottman.com/about/the-gottman-method/ and
   https://www.gottman.com/about/research/

http://www.huffingtonpost.com/50

http://www.infoplease.com/

http://www.marc.ucla.edu/

http://www.mylifestylecareer.com/

http://www.nextavenue.org

http://www.theneuroticparent.com/

https://www.psychologytoday.com/

Video

Brown, Brené. "The Power of Vulnerability." Filmed June 2010. TED video, 20:19. https://www.ted.com/talks/brene_brown_on_vulnerability.

The Ellen Degeneres Show. "Madonna, The Cast of 'One Big Happy.'" September 2, 2015. http://www.ellentv.com/episodes/madonna-week -begins-the-cast-of-one-big-happy/.

Interviews

Mithra Ballesteros, Beverly Beckham, Karen Blessing, Linda and Charlie Bloom, Louise Cady-Fernandes, Lisa Carpenter, Carol Fishman Cohen, Nancy Collamer, Dr. Richard Davidson, Laura Ehlers, Becky Galli, Dr. Barbara Greenberg, Sharon Hodor Greenthal, Mary Dell Harrington, Dr. Jennifer L. Hartstein, Beth Havey, Lois Hoffman, Kay Williams, Laura Ann Klein, Dr. Irene S. Levine, Danyelle Smith Little, Georgette Adrienne Lopez, Roseanne McAlear, Doreen McGettigan, Josann McGibbon, Winifred White Neisser, Risa Nye, Ellen Orlando, Sara Parriott, Jane Pauley, Dr. Carl Pickhardt, Yvonne Ransel, J.D. Rothman, Dr. Margaret Rutherford, Candy Schulman, Andrea Seppinni, Janine Talbot, Mindy Klapper Trotta, Lisa Stapleton Weldon, Michele Willens.

ACKNOWLEDGMENTS

This book was a labor of love for the sisterhood of mothers. It would not have been possible without you.

Special thanks to my agent Carol Mann, and Lydia Blyfield of the Carol Mann Agency; the wonderful people at Sourcebooks: Michelle Lecuyer, Anna Michels, Shana Drehs, Becca Sage, Connie Gabbert, Sabrina Baskey, Cassie Gutman, Angela Cardoz, and Michelle Dellinger; to Shelley Emling at *Huff/Post50* for featuring the essays in my series every week, without fail; to Jim Donovan for your generosity, guidance, and friendship; to my family: Steven Shultz, Nicholas Shultz, Alexander Shultz, Peter Shultz, Luis Rodriguez, Jessie Tromberg, Bruce Tromberg, Patti Tromberg, Alicia Kuttner, Joshua Tromberg, Matthew Tromberg, and Daniel Tromberg, for making my life fuller and richer; to my father, whom I miss every day; to my aunts and uncles, Martha and Fred Tromberg and Arlene and Bob Bein, for making me feel loved, sharing your experiences, and for listening carefully; to John Darrouzet, for your exuberance and for being an original; and to Roseanne McAlear, one of the smartest, funniest women I've ever had the pleasure of calling my friend.

My eternal thanks to everyone who generously contributed to *From Mom to Me Again*, including: Mithra Ballesteros, Beverly Beckham, Karen Blessing, Linda and Charlie Bloom, Louise Cady-Fernandes, Lisa Carpenter, Carol Fishman Cohen, Nancy Collamer, Dr. Richard Davidson, Laura Ehlers, Becky Galli, Lisa J. Goins, Dr. Barbara Greenberg, Sharon Hodor Greenthal, Mary Dell Harrington, Dr. Jennifer L. Hartstein, Beth Havey, Lisa Heffernan, Lois Hoffman, Kay Williams, Laura Ann Klein, Dr. Irene S. Levine, Danyelle Smith Little, Georgette Adrienne Lopez, Roseanne McAlear, Doreen McGettigan, Josann McGibbon, Winifred White Neisser, Risa Nye, Ellen Orlando, Daniel Ostroff, Sara Parriott, Anne Parris, Jane Pauley, Dr. Carl Pickhardt, Vivian Steir Rabin, Yvonne Ransel, J. D. Rothman, Dr. Margaret Rutherford, Candy Schulman, Andrea Seppinni, Jill Smokler, Janine Talbot, Mindy Klapper Trotta, Lisa Stapleton Weldon, and Michele Willens; the Texas "Motherload"; my sweet pal Benji; and editor Nancy Luse, who published my first essays in the *Frederick News Post* when my nest was newly full. Finally, to the house on the hill, which gave my children a place to dream; and to Starbucks' pumpkin bread, hot green tea, and the baristas at my favorite store, #6579, who make me feel like Norm on *Cheers*.

Thank you all.

Melissa T. Shultz

ABOUT THE AUTHOR

Melissa T. Shultz has written about health and parenting for the *New York Times*, the *Washington Post*, the *Dallas Morning News*, *Newsweek*, *Readers' Digest*, *Huffington Post*, *Next Avenue*, Scarymommy.com, Babble .com, and other publications and blogs. She is also an acquisitions editor for Jim Donovan Literary. A native of Washington, DC, and mother of two sons, she now lives in the Dallas area with her husband.